Foreword by **Dr. RT Kendall**

WHY NOT YOU?

An Invitation to a Spirit-Led Life,
Reaching Everyone, Everywhere, Everyday

Waleed Zarou

Copyright © 2024 Waleed Zarou
ISBN: 979-8-8693-0160-4
Published in the United States of America

All rights reserved. No part of this book may be used or reproduced by any means, graphic, electronic, or mechanical, including photocopying, recording, taping or by any information storage retrieval system without the written permission of the publisher except in the case of brief quotations embodied in critical articles and reviews.

Original Version
Copyright © 2023 by Waleed Zarou
ISBN: 9798392530519
Library of Congress Registration: 2023908935

Unless otherwise marked, Scripture is taken from the *New King James Version*®. Copyright © 1982 by Thomas Nelson. Used by permission. All rights reserved.

Scripture quotations marked with NIV, are taken from THE HOLY Bible, NEW INTERNATIONAL VERSION®, NIV® Copyright © 1973, 1978, 1984, 2011 by Biblica, Inc.® Used by permission. All rights reserved worldwide.

Scripture quotations marked KJV are taken from *The King James Version of The Holy Bible*. Public domain.

Scripture quotations marked NLT are taken from THE HOLY BIBLE, NEW LIVING TRANSLATION, copyright © 1996, 2004, 2015 by Tyndale House Foundation. Used by permission of Tyndale House Publishers, Inc., Carol Stream, Illinois 60188. All rights reserved.

Scripture quotations a marked ESV are taken from *The Holy Bible, English Standard Version*®), copyright © 2001 by Crossway, a publishing ministry of Good News Publishers. Used by permission. All rights reserved.

Bedford, Texas

Dedication

I can only dedicate this book to my beautiful wife, Amy. Thank you for becoming one, praying, laughing, crying, joking, loving, advising, working, serving, giving, traveling, and doing every part of life with me—you're a gift to me, our children, the body of Christ, and to this world. You make me smile and everyone who meets you. Your voice lifted up to God daily in worship always inspires me to love Jesus more! I love you.

Acknowledgments

"A chain is no stronger than its weakest link" (Thomas Reid). Many of us have heard that to express the ability of a person or group to be successful. The success of an entire group depends on the success of each individual member of the group. If one person fails, then they all do. When you look at people that have succeeded in life, it is often because of all that the team put into that person. It's so true in the Kingdom. It all starts with God's redemptive plan and the people He puts in our lives—those we become a part of each other's lives to accomplish God's purposes. You'll also find no one is successful or becomes a man of God without the ministry of others to him and around him. This is why I feel exceptionally humbled and blessed to have the people involved in my life that I do.

Starting with my own family, my wife Amy, and my daughters Juliana, Nina, and Sophia, whom I have learned so much and still do from being husband and father to. You all hold the keys to my heart and will always be Daddy's heartthrob! Thank you for surrounding me with your love even in the hardest times.

To Mr. Tate, the missionary who I never met. Who came from America to reach my grandfather with the gospel truth on the coast of Palestine in the early 1900s. My grandfather's life was ever changed from this man's obedience to leave his natural comforts to tell others what Jesus had done for the whole world.

Thank you, Grandpa, for receiving the love of Jesus and being faithful to walk with him for another 50 years. Your prayers were effective and powerful for so many years until you were able to see the first grandchild born of the Spirit. My mom, who loved and served us, died young. I miss and love you.

Thank you, Dad, for all your sacrifice, support, and example of working hard every day to serve your family. Thank you for coming back to Jesus at 71 and living your last 11 years as a hero to me. I miss you all and can't wait to see you in Heaven.

I also want to acknowledge my brother Ron, who was the first to accept Christ and pick up his grandfather's mantle. You continue to be an example of what a faithful man of God should be. I am eternally grateful for your friendship and honored to be your brother. Thank you for praying and loving me.

I offer special thanks to pastor Dale O'Shields for obeying the Spirit to visit and challenge me that day at our family's pizzeria. He knows what I'm referring to for giving an altar call message to be born again after all your sermons. I was first unchained in the high school auditorium you were renting when the church was still starting.

Thank you, Pastor Star Scott, who became my spiritual father and mentor two months after being born again in 1989. Your example of cutting a straight path to the truth and uncompromised obedience to God's word, no matter what circumstances and opposition you faced, continues to teach me how to grow in my sonship and answer the call of God in humility.

Thanks to all my friends who continue to support, pray, and live as examples of the believer in word and deed consistently for many years.

I want to thank Cory Edwards for all her administrative support. Also, Lynn Carr for her vigorous editing efforts. Samantha Lorsitch for her amazing cover design work and creative input.

Another special thanks go to my friend Tim Synan, who coached and advised me on so many things to help me with getting this book completed and distributed.

Also, I thank Tim Taylor, who has spoken vision into the book and its development. His maturity and years of experience writing so many books for his father, Jack Taylor, and others have been evident from the start of this process until the end. I look forward to what lies ahead for us both.

All these mentioned, and so many others, have contributed to the start and completion of this book and making sure that I am a strong link in a part of this big team called the Body of Christ. Like Paul said, "I am what I am by the grace of God," expressed to me through all these gifted people in my life. If there is any success with this book, it will be because of all these people God has sent to help me. Without any of them, I would not be a strong team member. All glory and honor to Jesus and His team!

Contents

Dedication	
Acknowledgments	
Foreword by RT Kendall	9
See What God Can Do	11
My Story	15
God's Heart for the Lost	27
A Compassionate Heart	39
The Gospel Clear and Simple	51
Going in Power	65
Lifestyle Evangelism	81
Reaching Our Neighbors & Coworkers	95
Follow Up Making Disciples	107
Time to Step Up The Spirit @ Work	121
About the Author	

Foreword

I met Waleed at a conference where I was speaking near D.C. He is a friend of a dear friend. I was impressed with him immediately for his poise and passion for reaching the lost. He told me he was writing a book, but little did I know it would make such an impact. Why Not You? is a masterpiece of a practical, personal, and simple approach to sharing the Gospel.

Waleed begins by raising your expectations—your faith—to see what God can not only do through you but what He desires to do with you. He tells his own story of being angry with God and how the mercy of the Father overwhelmed him to turn from a murderous soul to a compassionate heart for other people. In his conversion, he gained God's heart for those running from Him, like he did.

He presents a compelling appeal for keeping the presentation of the Gospel simple and direct. His relational approach to leading people to Jesus has proven effective in his life and is easily transferable if one is willing to let God be God in your life. This book is full of examples of how God has used Waleed to bring others to Jesus. It is a lifestyle that is easily copied and very contagious.

Not to imply that the approach Waleed presents is a matter of his talents or hard work, he readily points the reader to the absolute necessity of the power of the Holy Spirit to transform lives. Not willing to settle for mere numerical growth, Waleed is committed to imparting to others the mandate to bring converts to maturity in Christ. His stated goal for evangelism is discipleship, not simply conversion.

Maybe the most exciting aspect of Why Not You? is the call to be a part of the harvest of souls that is coming by the will of God. Evangelism is the mission of every believer, and every believer is empowered to do it. This book is an invitation for everyone everywhere, every day, to be the light of God in this dark world. Nothing is stopping us from fulfilling the Great Commission except our willingness to obey and walk in the power of the Holy Spirit to reach our family, friends, neighbors, coworkers, customers, and even strangers with the wonderful message of transformation through Jesus Christ.

Waleed presents a simple plan and welcomes you to join him in doing and being the will of God where you work, live, and play. Read this book! Read this book to receive the motivation to go. Read this book to increase your expectations and faith in what God can do through you. Read this book to gain an ally in the war for the souls of men and women worldwide. Remember, we win! Coming to Christ is inevitable! How people come is the only question. Read this book to be part of the loving army of God that intentionally welcomes lives into the Kingdom like a farmer harvests his field.

RT Kendall

See What God Can Do

Our companies, jobs, and professions give us access, and access gives us opportunity for Kingdom impact on the lives of people who may not normally come to church or hear the Gospel otherwise.

After completing a bachelor's degree from the University of Maryland and working in the corporate world, I went to trade school and interned at some of the top salons and hair cutting shops in my area. At barber school, a friend of my father's, a longtime barber, took me under his wing. After two months, he said, "I can't teach you anymore. I'm done with you. You're ready to go out on your own." My life was full of experiences of meeting people along the way who helped me advance to reach my goals.

After returning from the mission field, I prayed and fasted for three days about what direction God had for me. I wanted to work in the top shops in the area, but the Lord had me open up a small shop in Tyson's Corner called International Barbers. It had four chairs and was sustained by some of the same people that influenced my father. I was determined that the business would serve my family and ministry, not the other way around. I even planned to shut the business down at the right time as the Lord led. I made a covenant with God about how to do this and how not to let the business get ahead of me. I arranged it as a tool for evangelistic outreach. Pastors from my church helped me dedicate the place for outreach to bring glory to the Lord. God blessed it. For ten years, the Lord had me in Tyson's Corner, reaching some of the wealthiest men (whom I call "up-and-outers") in the world. Founders, senior executives, and owners from some of the largest companies in our country were my clients. Many clients worked at some of the most prestigious accounting and law firms. Through the services we provided, we ministered to them while they were in our chairs. I've seen several of these men weep over concerns in their lives under the conviction of the Holy Spirit. The chair was an opportunity to get to know these men and for them to get to know themselves. I simply loved them and pointed them to Jesus. We did a great job in our profession, but the purpose of the business was to preach the Gospel.

Several Christians wanted to work at the business with me. I told them, "This is not a normal shop. If you don't see your chair as a pulpit, this is not the right place for you. If you're not going to evangelize, I will fire you for not sharing Jesus here. Evangelism is what we do here."

Of course, skill and professionalism were basic presumptions. Christians can be the best at what they do. In fact, they must seek to be the best at what they do. Success is credibility. If you don't do a good job, why would anyone do business with you? I was passionate about sharing Christ through my profession. I would say, "If you just want a comfortable place to hide out and call yourself a Christian, then I recommend you work somewhere else."

Not everyone is equipped to preach at work at first, but if you're willing to learn, you can become quite adept at preaching the Gospel and being a top professional. Some had the heart to learn, and we showed them how they could preach Jesus to everyone every day through their lives right where they were. There was one young lady whom we discipled by encouraging her through a hard time. She saw what we were doing, and she loved it. She was a great hairdresser and a powerful witness for Jesus Christ. She's in the ministry today. Even when I wanted to sell the business and go back to the mission field, the Lord was teaching me that where you are is your mission field. That job was where God wanted me to be at that time. Everyone can be a missionary, but not everyone can go overseas. If you can't win souls here, you're not going to win them overseas. A missionary is someone who is a Christian everywhere, every day. What is a missionary? Missionaries are simply normal Christians who live in another country. Be a missionary at home first!

The burden for home missions kept growing in my heart. I saw the pain of the up-and-outers who were my customers. The book of Proverbs says a man's gift makes room for him and brings him before great men. There's no way I could have met and served those people without God's help. Without that platform of my business, I would never have met those people. For ten years, God had me in that shop in Tyson's Corner. The business was also a platform for teaching other believers to do the same. I saw the Holy Spirit use others to do some miraculous things in people's lives.

I maintain many of those relationships even today. I have asked the Lord why He hasn't sent me back there, but He continues to use me wherever I go. I do not want to get ahead of the Lord. I am learning to be content by staying in my lane, but evangelism is my lifestyle everywhere, every day. I was able to share the Gospel with hundreds of people in those ten years. I know they heard the Gospel right there in my chair. I don't know how many people might have come to faith in Christ, all because of that little hole-in-the-wall shop.

Think of what could happen if believers did something similar across the country or even the world. What if all Christians across the country used their businesses as a platform to preach the Good News of Jesus Christ? I like to call it "Kingdom business." Deuteronomy 8:18 says it is God who gives us the power to attain wealth. The ability to attain wealth and the motive to succeed come from God so we can establish His covenant. He desires to use us to establish and complete His purposes and plans. We don't get rich just to sit on yachts and drive a Mercedes. There's nothing wrong with prosperity if God has given it to us, but at the same time, we are to seek Him and put Him first. If we seek Him first, all we need will follow us (Matthew 6:33). The pursuit of being rich can be a danger. It is the love of money, instead of people, that is the downfall of so many (2 Timothy 6:10). God desire to use you to reap His harvest of souls before His Son comes again. Imagine what God can do with you!

My Story

My story of following Jesus began before I was thinking about God. I had a godly grandfather who came to faith in Christ in the early 1900s in Jaffa, where he grew up south of Tel Aviv in Israel. American missionaries had reached him with the Gospel. Although my family was Palestinian, we were never Muslim. Our heritage goes back to the second or third century during Roman persecution in the Gulf area and what is modern-day Yemen. Our ancestors migrated north and settled in Palestine. My lineage was comprised of neither Muslims nor born-again believers. The general understanding of salvation by faith and grace in Christ alone was dominated by more traditional Roman Catholic and Greek or Eastern Orthodox influence in the generations of my family. In the early 1900s, a man named Mr. Tate shared the Gospel with Grandpa. Grandpa became a follower of Jesus, serving God for fifty years. He was a powerful man of God—a man of prayer. I was told that Mr. Tate prayed up to eight hours a day. He walked in the Spirit. My grandfather was a man full of faith. He pastored a church for twenty years in Ramallah on the West Bank. When he grew too old, he turned the church over to a younger man. Then my dad brought him to live with us in Rockville, Maryland.

The Prayers of My Grandfather

As a child, I remember thinking my grandfather was a strange man. He prayed for us for thirty years before the first family member, my brother Ron (Pastor Ron today), came to faith in Christ. Ron's conversion eventually led me to become a follower of Christ, but it was Grandpa's intercession for thirty years that made it all happen. Before he died, he told my brother he had been praying for the family for thirty years and that Ron was the first to come to faith in Christ. Grandpa told him, "More are coming." He said he had seen them already. When I consider the verse from the Book of James, "The effectual, fervent prayer of a righteous man avails much," I think of my grandpa and his intercession for us. His name was Peter Zarou. In Arabic, "Peter" is "Boutros," similar to the Greek "Pétros." He told my brother, "You're the first. I've prayed for thirty years. You're the first, but I have seen others coming too." He had strong faith. Faith is when we stop believing what we see and start seeing what we believe. When I think of faith, I think of Grandpa. He saw what he believed. His faith compelled him to pray to see souls in his family come to Christ.

My brother Ron was the first to convert. He was a very gifted, hardworking athlete, and he was committed to basketball. He was on a recruiting visit to UCLA when his trip was abruptly cut short. I didn't know why, but when he got home, he talked about Jesus Christ. I thought it was very odd. What I didn't know was that Ron was meeting with friends of my grandfather. My grandfather had plugged into Halpine Baptist Church in Rockville for fellowship and ministry. He would assist the pastor from time to time. Thank God for that pastor!

My dad's barbershop was the epicenter of the old town of Rockville, Maryland. Everybody who was anybody in the area came to my dad's shop. Grandpa's friends would share the Gospel with my dad there. My brother connected with one of them and started asking a lot of questions about what it meant to be a Christian. I didn't know he was searching for Jesus. He mainly talked to my dad about it. My dad, being a backslider at the time, told him Christianity was the truth. He seemed to know the Christian life is the hardest life to live, but it is the true way to live. My dad shared that he was once really devoted to walking with God as a young man, but he had gotten off track. Shortly after that, my brother converted. I thought he went mad. I thought evangelical fundamentalists who talked about born-again Christianity were absolute wackos.

The Mission of Revenge

I was eighteen years old. I had just shut down a small international drug ring I was running in the US with connections to Colombia. A few of my cousins and friends worked for me. I did that during my junior and senior years of high school in Rockville at Richard Montgomery High School. I carried a loaded 9-millimeter in an Italian Benelli holster with sixteen hollow-point rounds in the clip. I never had an issue with any of the students. It was for protection from other drug dealers. Everyone knew where to find me, so I felt responsible for protecting those around me. I carried a gun and would not have hesitated to use it. This was my job and my mindset.

WHY NOT YOU?

During my high school years, my brother had his encounter with God. I didn't realize what was going on. I figured he had lost his mind, or somebody messed him up. I thought to myself, "No one can do this to my brother and get away with it. You can't mess with my family like this." I was already an angry young man, very bitter toward life. I was looking for a scapegoat to blame for my troubles. I flew 3,000 miles to Los Angeles to find this street preacher I thought had ruined my brother by converting him to Christ. On the plane, I was thinking that this was the right thing to do. I was going to kill this man. Instead of thinking murder was wrong, I thought killing him was justified. My plane landed, and I headed for Westwood, California, where I thought this preacher hung out. In the eighties, Westwood was a big hangout for everybody. It is still currently a very popular area.

I got to that part of town around midnight and walked a two-mile square radius back and forth, looking for this guy. I didn't find him the first night. It actually took me two months to find my target, but when I did, everything went black. There he was, a street preacher, a young man, probably close to my age, holding a Bible and preaching on the street. I didn't act right away. I got myself a job in the neighborhood working at a pizza shop so I could be close to where he was. I came out one Friday night at midnight, and I saw the young man preaching. It was a packed Friday night; people were hanging out everywhere. He was boldly proclaiming the Word of God in the street. Some people were listening, and others were angry. For me, it was instant hatred. Looking back at it now, I believe I had some demonic influence. I remember everything turning black. I wanted to kill him with the pleasure of using just my bare hands, no weapons. I wasn't on drugs or alcohol or anything like that. I didn't need it. I was already crazy without it. I made a beeline for him, and everything turned black. Whatever was between him and me, I charged right through it. I don't remember feeling it, but I know I walked through people. When I got about seven or eight feet from him, it was like I hit a brick wall. There was no real wall to be seen, but it stopped me in my tracks.

Suddenly, my soul was deeply gripped with a fear like I had never known before. Up to this point, as an eighteen-year-old, I'd had several near-death experiences because of my violence. I was given to violence and had been in several life-and-death situations. I knew what fear was, but I did not know what happened as I neared this street preacher to kill him. Something gripped my soul from the inside out. The best way I can describe it is that God grabbed my soul and squeezed it. I was immediately stopped and, at that moment, made aware that I was not opposing a man. I was not coming against a person; I was opposing God Himself. It shook me to my very core. To this day, I can't cease wondering how although I was not thinking about God, He was thinking about me! I had no idea what He saw in me because I had nothing to give or offer God but fear, darkness, shame, guilt, and rebellion. It's impossible even to consider. It reminds me of what Jesus said while they were crucifying Him. He said, "Father, forgive them. They don't know what they're doing." His executioners weren't asking for forgiveness; neither was I. I didn't even know I needed God at the time, let alone think about forgiveness or ask for it.

All my problems in life—all my bitterness, hatred, and anger—were exposed in that one moment. My beef was with God, and He was not pleased. I felt an immediate fear that I could die at that moment, and it would be righteous. I used to fight a lot. I boxed a little competitively, but I fought much more outside the boxing ring. It felt like God hit me with a right cross that rocked the foundation of my soul. I didn't know Jesus yet, but I walked away with my head down, wondering what just happened. I walked and walked seven miles, all the way to Santa Monica. I had missed the last bus to take me back to Santa Monica from LA, so I had a long two-and-a-half-hour walk back to where I was staying. When I got back to the room I was renting in Santa Monica, I was stunned by what had happened to me. I flew back to the East Coast as soon as I could. My mom was upset I had been gone for so long, not knowing I was going to California. She was worried. I felt like my mission was a failure. What I went there to do didn't happen. I thought about staying out there but decided to go back to junior college. I was enrolled in Montgomery College in Rockville, Maryland, and completed the semester.

When I got back to school, two young born-again believers approached me on campus as I walked to the library. I was going to study, but they stopped me and asked if they could share the Gospel with me. They had that look in their eyes, and I knew they were the real thing. They looked like nerds, but they had something I knew I didn't have. Whatever it was, it commanded my respect. They began to talk about the Bible. I cut them off and said, "Hey, wait a minute, I think my brother became one of you guys." They laughed. I said, "I'm not sure about all this Bible stuff. I think the Bible might have contradictions in it. I'm just not sure." They said, "Sir, can we ask you a question?" I said, "Yeah." They asked, "Have you ever read the Bible?" I had to say, "No." It's like they took my foot and put it right in my mouth. These guys looked at me and said, "We see you're not ready." They had good discernment, and they did not force it. They said, "Can we leave you with something?" They left me with a wonderful Gospel tract that I've been sharing with others for the past thirty years. It's called "Missing Heaven by 18 Inches." I couldn't throw it away. I was under immense conviction, and I went to my car later and read the whole tract. It's a powerful Gospel tract that presents the average American as being eighteen inches away from heaven because although he believes in Christ in his mind, he has not received Him (Jesus Christ) as personal Lord in his heart. The average distance between the brain and the heart is eighteen inches. I couldn't forget that.

I have heard that the average person hears the Gospel six and a half times before they receive the truth of it. I was finally getting it. That was my first encounter with the actual Gospel message. I still had a lot of questions. The most powerful impact was seeing my brother's life change. I knew God Himself somehow changed my brother; he had encountered God. I knew my brother very well, so I knew he hadn't just joined a social club. He was different. I couldn't deny it. The things he used to love; he stopped loving. The things he used to hate; he started to like. He began to live to honor and please God in everything he said and did. That was evident. I was trying to understand. I'm not sure if I liked it, but he was still my brother. I still was very protective of him. I know he took a lot of ridicule and mockery from cousins, friends, and several family members. These were people who called themselves Christians. They were baptized. They would say, "We're from Jerusalem. What are you going to tell us about Jesus?" He dealt with that religious, Pharisaical attitude from day one. My dad remained silent through it all. He knew my brother was walking in the truth. He was a preacher's kid. He knew better. It was affecting me, and I started asking a lot of questions.

Questions for God

I had three main questions. First, Is Jesus really who He said He was? He was not claiming to be a prophet or even just a Bible teacher: He was claiming to be God, a deity. I thought, "This guy is either a nutcase, the biggest scam on humanity, or He is who He said He was." God became a man—I didn't think that would be impossible. If God wanted to be a man, He could do that. He could do whatever He wanted to do if He was all-powerful. I believed that, especially after my experience in California. He stopped me from killing that guy. If Jesus was who He said He was, I had to rethink my whole life. I was pretty much a humanist at the time. I believed that all roads ultimately led to heaven and that if you were a good person, your path would eventually lead to God. There are so many different religions because people don't know better. Jesus was claiming inclusivity (that everyone is welcome). But He also claimed He was the only way, the truth, and the life, that no one could or would come to God except through Him. That was my first question: "Is Jesus who He said He is?"

The second question was, "What does being 'born again' mean? My brother would show me the Gospel of John, where Jesus said a man must be born again, or he will not see the kingdom of God. It said, "cannot"— "will not." That bothered me. I used to ask my brother, "Hey, is everyone who's not born again not going to go to heaven? How can God do that? What kind of God is He, a God of wrath and anger?" I had just experienced some of His wrath and anger.

The third question was, Is the Bible God's book? Is it the truth? Is it really what it claims to be? Because I hadn't looked at it yet, this provoked me. I started going weekly to Catholic catechism classes. These people claimed to be the direct representatives of Jesus Christ on the planet. I said, "These guys are the Dons of religion. Maybe they are God's representatives. They're powerful. They claim to be direct descendants of Peter, and they have the truth." I put my college studies aside and began looking at their claims in the catechism books. I also compared these claims to the Bible, back and forth, for about three weeks, sometimes up to sixteen hours a day. Some of the things the Catholic Church professed were Biblical and good. Other things seemed to directly oppose what the Scripture said. I thought to myself, "Either they're right, and the Bible is wrong, or the Bible is right, and they are wrong." Both can't be right. I found some errors. When there was a conflict with the Scripture, the Catholic Church would revert to the interpretation of some Church Father or elevate its interpretation above the Word. That bothered me.

I met with a regional bishop in the church and visited most of the many Catholic churches in Rockville. I was genuinely under conviction, sincerely trying to change and make myself a better person. I was searching! I had a hole in my heart; I was empty, and the hole kept getting bigger and bigger. I was the type of guy whose every third word was profanity in English, Arabic, and sometimes other languages. I could be extremely violent. If someone crossed me, I would be very mean to them. I broke people's faces for looking at me wrong. It got worse. Sin does not remain neutral. Sin takes us further than we planned to go, keeps us longer than we want to stay, and costs us more than we are willing to pay. I was no exception. I knew I was living in deep sin. I met with a priest, and he put me in touch with the bishop of the regional diocese at St. Jude's on Veirs Mill Road. After I met with him, I was done with the Catholic Church. He told me that God's love lived in me already. He did not show me anything from the Bible or back up his words with quotes from the Bible. I became extremely angry. I thought he was making fun of me. Under extreme conviction, I knew I was a sinner on my way to hell. He was trying to tell me that God's love was in me. I got mad. I walked away and said, "Thank you. I'm done." I knew the devil was in control of me, and I was not living for God, so how could this man tell me God's love was in me, such a great sinner?

I called my brother and asked him, "Can you send me a Bible? Can you find me a man of God? Are there any men left in the area who fear God enough to tell the truth and not worry about what people think? Is anyone more concerned with what God says than what people say? Are there any men left like that?" I can't share the words I used to graphically describe that priest. I could hear my brother chuckling. He was back in Virginia then and said, "You're asking a hard thing, but give me some time." There was a man named Pastor Dale O'Shields on the radio. My brother told me later that he thought, "This guy sounds like he has a pretty good word on him. Let me send Waleed there." My brother drove all the way from Virginia and gave me an NIV Bible, and I started reading it at night. I was reading the words of Jesus, and they were messing me up. The message that messed me up the most was the one my brother shared with me all the time: "You can't have two masters. If you love one, you will hate the other. Either you are for Me, or you are against Me." I knew where I was; I knew I was against God. Now that I saw it from the Scriptures with the words of Christ, it messed me up even more. In some ways, the truth of Scripture was tormenting me.

I tried harder to change myself. I was training twice a day, boxing and working out in the gym. I was working at my family business and was in school at the University of Maryland. I had a crazy schedule. I was being tormented by the truth daily. I had endless energy. I'd ride my bike for a workout before I went to the gym. I would ride five, six, seven, or even eight miles to a Catholic church and go into the sanctuary. I would sneak around, making sure no one was looking, and dunk my whole face in the holy water.

At night I would get in trouble. I had no power over sin in my life. All this was tormenting me more. It was intensifying. One time I tried to stop cursing. I was so proud of myself. I didn't use profanity for two months.

Then something happened in our restaurant. One of my employees mouthed off at me, and sure enough, I grabbed the mop, ready to smash his head. I was blurting out curse words in Arabic and English for about two minutes nonstop. God, in His mercy, once again stopped me on the spot. God didn't have to stop me from killing a man or being killed by other life-threatening situations I was in. He didn't owe me anything. If God had punished me for everything I did during that time or any time, it would have been just. After cursing him out, I heard a voice say, "What's in your heart comes out of your mouth." I had just read that scripture the night before! I heard the voice of God in my head say, "You're trying to change the outside. I want your heart." I heard God's voice just like that—just that clearly. God's voice called me just like that. I thought to myself, "That means surrendering everything. I don't know if I'm ready to surrender everything. I don't want to be a hypocrite. I don't respect hypocrites."

One night, after a long day at work, I was sitting out behind the restaurant. The stars were shining, and I looked up and heard the Spirit of God say, "Come unto Me all ye that are heavy laden, and I'll give you rest. My Yoke is easy" (Matthew 11). I'd wrestle with it and ask, "You want me to come to You? Do you know how great a sinner I am? I've done some wicked stuff, Lord. How do you want me to come to you?" Like Peter when he said, "Lord, depart from me. I'm a wicked man." I was under such great conviction. I didn't want to surrender. I didn't want to give up my womanizing.

So, at the age of twenty-two, I visited the pastor and church my brother had recommended, the Church of the Redeemer. At the time, they were meeting in the auditorium of Gaithersburg High School. Currently, they have multiple campuses in Maryland. Five hundred people were there. I was dating Miss Maryland USA then, and she came with me. When they gave an altar call, I tried slipping out. I had to get back across town to open the restaurant because Sunday was my day to open the family pizzeria. I don't know what happened. I turned around, hit the aisle, and the next thing I knew, the pastor was in front of me, shaking my hand. I thought, "How'd he get here so fast? How did he even spot me?" "Hello, young man. My name is Pastor Dale O'Shields. Nice to meet you," he said. He had that little look in his eye. He said, "What do you do?" Since hospitality is a big part of our culture, it was very natural for me to invite him to visit when he asked what I did. I replied, "My family owns a business across town. If you're around, please come by." For me, to show up to church was huge. I was not playing games because I knew it was all or nothing with God. I was under such conviction, 24/7. I knew my day of surrender was around the corner. I could hear God calling me and feel Him pulling me to Himself.

Two days after that church service, I was wrestling with God, saying, "This is my week to surrender." In the restaurant with my apron on that day, I looked up and guess who I saw pulling up. He could park right up front because the restaurant was in a strip mall. As the pastor and his wife were pulling up, I was thinking, "Oh my goodness!" I knew God had sent him. "O Lord, You're after me. You sent them here." I welcomed them and seated them. They like calzones. It is still, to this day, the biggest calzone I've ever made for anybody in my life. He was very kind, as was his wife. They sat in a booth as I rehearsed my history with them. I told them about my family—my grandfather being a pastor and evangelist and my brother now a follower of Christ. Pastor Dale was a very soft-spoken man, and in the natural, I didn't have a lot of regard for people like that. If you have something to say, say it, is the way I thought. That was my personality, the way I was—very direct. The Spirit of God in him changed. He turned and looked at me. It was like he turned into a little lion. He squared up in my face and said, "Quit the small talk, son. Have you ever made a public profession of Jesus Christ as your personal Lord and Savior?" I swallowed hard. I knew it was God speaking through him. I looked at him and said, "Yes, Sir. One time I did in a mockery, making fun of Christians." "Yeah, well, you need to do it for real. It's your time," he replied. I swallowed hard again. I knew that was God's voice. I said, "Sir, you're right. God sent you here, and I'll be the first one down the altar this Sunday. Pastor, I'll be wearing my tennis shoes." Those weren't cheap words to me.

Sunday came, and I had the first vision I've ever had in my life. I've had only three visions in thirty years, and that was the first. I don't remember what the pastor preached. I didn't hear one word of the whole sermon. I was waiting for him to give me the invitation. To this day, that pastor gives invitations after every service. When he gave the invitation, and I went to stand up, I felt like something slammed me down on my chair. "What's going on?" I wondered. The scripture that tormented me for years came back to me: "You can't have two masters. Either you are for Me or against Me; you will love one and hate the other." I wondered, "Why is this so hard?" In my vision, I saw myself on my knees with chains on my wrists and ankles, bowing in front of Satan. It was a vision of what my life had been. I said, "No, no more." I stood up, and I hit the aisle. As soon as I did, all those chains fell off. I felt freedom like I never had. I had tried to be religious before. I tried to burn candles in front of images of Christ and pray. It was all to no avail. It was nothing like this. All my chains fell off right there. I experienced immediate freedom. I went down to the altar, and another couple was there. The pastor and his wife asked, "Would you like to pray? Do you want us to pray with you?" For the first time, I knew God was listening; I had His ear and His heart. I said, "No, I'd like to pray." I prayed, "Father, don't ever let my pride get in the way of knowing You or following You again." That was it. I was immediately changed. I left that church a new man. I went back to the shop. The birds were singing; the sky was brighter. It was like a Disney movie. I felt like a new man in Jesus.

That day, my coworker was a backslidden Christian. Just two weeks before, I had tried to kill him. He had snapped off at me, and I remember chasing him to his car, trying to take a mop handle to crush his head open. He got away—thank God! I went in the restaurant, and he was the first guy I saw. I told him, "Hey, I gave my life to Jesus today. You won't believe what happened to me, Richie. I want to ask you to forgive me for what I did to you last week. Please forgive me. I'm sorry about it." He looked at me and said, "What happened to you?" I said, "God is awesome; He set me free." I'm on the biggest high I've ever had in my life. That high didn't stop. A couple of months went by, and that young man plugged back into that church; he gave his life to the Lord again and stayed committed until the day he died. He went home to be with the Lord in his twenties. I don't know what killed him, but it was great that he got his life in order before he passed. I visited that church for another two months, and then the Lord led me to Calvary and Pastor Scott's ministry. I've been discipled there ever since.

Within two months of being saved, I led my first person to the Lord. He was a firefighter at the police/fire academy in Montgomery County. My brother and I had passes to work out at the academy gym. They had 24-hour security and let us use their weight room until midnight. This man was a big, thick, rusty-looking guy from Louisiana. God was moving in my life with a new zeal to lead people out of bondage like He had done for me. God was so merciful and gracious with me that I felt obligated to share the Gospel with everyone I met. If God could get my attention, He certainly can get yours. My story is the foundation for this book. God saved me from my horrible life in order to use me. Every experience I had; He has used for His glory. God did not gloss over my sin. He erased it. His mercy triumphed over justice in my life so He could use me to change other lives. I am an evangelist by gifting and calling. I am calling you, dear reader, to do the work of an evangelist. I pray this book will open your eyes to the white harvest that is out there. I am calling you to rise up and reap.

My story is also for leaders in the Church who have great influence. You see your congregation. You know your sheep. I am calling you to raise up evangelists in your midst to reap souls for Jesus. Recognize them, receive them, and release them into the harvest to see lives transformed. God has given you gifted people who need just a little training, a little nudge, to be who God created them to be. Find them.

My story is also for anyone who thinks he has messed up too much and feels God can't or won't use him. You cannot sin too much for God to change you and use you! My story is for anyone who is too fearful about surrendering everything to God. If God can save me and use me, He can do the same and greater with anyone else who is available.

God's Heart for the Lost

I want to turn now from sharing some of my personal testimony to sharing some practical content on evangelism. But first, a story.

Lady Florence Chadwick was one of the most accomplished swimmers of her day. She was the first woman to swim the English Channel in both directions. In 1951, she suffered a very disappointing failure. She had set out to swim from Catalina Island to Los Angeles, California, but she fell short of her goal. Several factors contributed to her defeat. First, as she began to swim, she noticed immediately that the water was unusually cold, numbing her limbs within a few minutes of entering the water. Second, a number of times during the swim, those accompanying her in the support boat had to fire shots to frighten sharks away. But perhaps the greatest obstacle was a dense fog that set in within a few hours of the swim. Lady Chadwick endured these obstacles for some time, but finally, she asked to be removed from the water. Her trainers begged her to continue. She complained, "I can't see the land." And she asked those with her, "Can you see the land?" The fog was so thick that no one could see how close she was to her goal. After she quit the swim in discouragement and exhaustion, she discovered she was only half a mile from the California coast, a distance easily reached under normal circumstances.

At a youth conference, she confessed, "I'm not excusing myself, but if I could have seen the coast, I think I could have made it." One year later, she completed that swim in record time. Do you think if Florence Chadwick had seen the land, she would have been able to kick out that last half mile? Absolutely! She would have conquered all obstacles in her way if her goal had been in sight.

As a follower of Jesus Christ, we can lose sight of the goal. We need a God's eye view. We need to know the bigger picture to complete the task of evangelism. Discovering God's heart for the lost will make us more effective in our evangelism. Knowing the goals of evangelism will prepare us to be tools for God to accomplish the desire of His heart. We cannot let the fog of life or conflict with the enemy distract us from following God's heart to reach the lost.

What is the goal of Biblical evangelism? Well, the goals of evangelism are fourfold.

The Goals of Evangelism

The first goal of Biblical evangelism is salvation. Evangelism, by its very definition, is sharing the Good News of Jesus Christ to lead another person to be born again. This is the first and primary goal. This is what Jesus said in John, Chapter 3. We must be born again! New birth is the foremost goal of Biblical evangelism.

Once a person is born again, the second goal of evangelism is discipleship. After leading them to the Lord, we want to see them baptized into a local church. We are baptized into His Body (visibly expressed in the local assembly of believers) by the Holy Spirit. Joining a local church is vital because the local body is where discipleship best takes place.

The third goal of Biblical evangelism is service. Every born-again believer is called to serve in the body. Becoming active members in a local church and exercising the gifts the Spirit has given to edify and strengthen one another is the ultimate goal of evangelism. Though this step may be the final step, it is not the end because service is to be continued for the rest of the believer's life. As believers mature, they become givers and even equippers as part of the process of discipleship. Salvation leads to discipleship; discipleship leads to service. Serving in the ministry of a local church is the final and ultimate goal of Biblical evangelism.

Biblical evangelism is more than leading someone to make a decision to follow Jesus. The commitment to believe in Jesus begins with a choice to reject the things of this world and follow Christ, but salvation is only the beginning. It is vital for newly born-again believers to get plugged into a local church to be discipled. The work of justification performed by the Lord requires the sanctification process worked out by the Holy Spirit. Discipleship is the program that leads a believer to mature and be used by God. Service, being used by God, is the ultimate goal of Biblical evangelism. Every Christian has a ministry. Not every follower of Christ is called to serve God vocationally, but every Christian is called to serve. Service requires maturity, and the process of discipleship never ends for the believer in Jesus Christ. We may be able to point to a day when we were saved, but we cannot name the date we will stop learning to be more like Jesus. We will spend eternity learning about God and His Kingdom, but it begins with salvation, leads to discipleship, and ends in service. Why are these steps not completed in every Christian's life? The biggest obstacle to completing the purpose of Biblical evangelism is the lack of knowledge of the long-term picture, the goals of God's heart. Christ said, "Teach them; go into all the world; preach the Gospel." The long-term picture doesn't stop when people become members of a local church. It's just the beginning of a life of serving and glorifying the Lord.

There is a fourth step embedded within the third goal of service. Disciples must become disciple-ers. The steps are not complete, and the job is unfinished until the disciple becomes a disciple-er. The cycle is not complete until the student matures to become a teacher. We often fall short of this because it is hard, and the fog gets in the way, obscuring the goal. Every believer is called to be a disciple-er.

In Hebrews 5, Paul is scolding his readers because they had not yet become teachers by this time in their lives in Christ. They had learned and experienced enough that they should have been instructing others to live like Jesus. Paul tells them it is time to move away from the elementary things and move on to maturity. We need to reiterate the goals of Biblical evangelism until our minds line up with the Scripture. Paul instructs us: "Let this mind be in you that was in Christ." To think Biblically is not condemning; it's something to be excited about. Scriptural correction is not about looking at yourself and admitting you've been doing this all wrong. Yesterday is past. We're not to stay in the past. We are not to condemn ourselves for things God has forgiven but to set our affections on things above. Today is a new day; today is the day the Lord has made. Let us rejoice in it and do His will today.

Christopher Columbus said, "You can never cross the ocean unless you have the courage to lose sight of the shore." Our feet are often too comfortable on land. When he sailed away from shore in the boat, he discovered something on the other side that the whole world said didn't exist. Once you and I are willing to get out of our comfort zones and get off the land where our feet feel comfortable, then we will see the things of God. We walk by faith, not by sight.

How do I get in the boat and let God take me where He wants me to be? Begin by knowing that there is someone to reach on the other side, hidden in the fog. A fog is hindering us from moving forward because we get too comfortable right where we are. There is nothing wrong with comfort—until it keeps us from being obedient. I am all for ease with no struggle, but unless I'm willing to get in the boat, I'm not going to discover what God has for me on the other side. I will never know who I'm going to meet and how God is going to use me unless I am willing to journey through the fog. As you pray, believe! Pray: "Father, make me a yielded vessel. Take me where You want me to go, Lord, because that's the only place I'll be satisfied to live."

This is the challenge. Believe and pray. Expect God to use you. Everyone makes mistakes along the way; none of us is perfect. We are all imperfect vessels who have been saved by grace. Go, yielded to His will. We are all growing from faith to faith. God will not beat us down for trying to do His will. Our obedience brings joy to Him. We are not responsible for the outcome; He is. He gives grace to us, grace to get back up when we fall down. If we never share the Gospel, we will never lead anyone to faith in Christ.

If we never lay hands on the sick and pray for them, we will never see answers to prayer. These are two guarantees. Faith works by love (Galatians 5:6). God's unconditional love for the person in front of us is what's important, not how intense my devotion time was today or how successful I feel today. God loves that person in front of you. He values him to the point of shedding the blood of His Son, Jesus. Jesus died for him. It is not about us. When you feel weak, confess it to God. "I feel weak. I don't feel spiritual. In fact, I feel slightly backslidden. I have been avoiding You for the past two days. I haven't been in Your Word." He knows already. That is not where we want to stay. Often, we get in God's way. Self-analysis creates spiritual paralysis. It keeps us behind the fog. We will not get to the other side until we look forward. Our feet will not leave the shore if we keep practicing self-analysis without obedience.

God is a missionary God. God is a sending God. "Missio Dei" is Latin and simply means "mission of God" or "sending of God." God is a saving God. God is a renewing God. He is a restoring God. He is a reconciling God. God sent His Son. He came to seek and save the lost (Luke 19:10). In the Garden, man fell. We know that man was separated from his relationship with God. As a result, man was filled with loneliness, anger, fear, selfishness, pain, sickness, pride, and all sorts of affliction. We can see the consequences of sin all around the world—disease, war, calamities, and all kinds of tragedies, both on a worldwide scale and in individual lives. No one is exempt from the wages of sin (Romans 6:27). Can you imagine going through whatever you've gone through in your life without Christ's being there, without the hope of God's help, care, and love? Unfortunately, too many do. Salvation was God's idea. He first loved us, and because God is love, we have a relationship with Him (1 John 4:8, 19).

Witnessing vs. Evangelism

I want to make a brief distinction here between witnessing and evangelizing. A witness represents who we are. Witnessing involves identity and defines who we are. We are witnesses of Christ. Witnessing is about how we live our lives and how we represent Jesus. This part is often more comfortable for many. The Holy Spirit was promised to empower us. Jesus told His disciples as He was leaving the earth, "You shall be My witnesses." Our witness is how we live; it's our lifestyle, who we are, and how we act. Compare this to evangelism, which is (very simply put), what we say. It's the proclamation or the preaching of the Good News. Christ said to go into all the world and preach the Good News. Preaching the Good News is evangelism.

Witnessing and evangelism go hand-in-hand. Our lifestyle should open the door to our preaching. I am familiar with the quote, "Preach the Gospel at all times. Use words if necessary" (often attributed to Francis of Assisi). Many Christians today understand evangelism to be the way we live as examples. Yes, we should exhibit Christlike character in all areas of our lives. But without using words to communicate the Gospel, we will never lead one person to turn from sin and put his faith in Christ. It is impossible to share the Gospel without words (Romans 10:14). Without words, people won't get saved. You need words to preach the Gospel. People need to hear the Good News so that they can receive it. It's faith in the Gospel that saves people. It's faith in what He said, "Repent and believe." Often, there is too much fuss about repentance versus believing, which one must happen first. We can dissect the heck out of it and miss the obvious. Repentance and belief are both required. We must change the way we think about God and receive Him. Believe who He is; He is the Savior. He is the Messiah. We must change what we think about God and then receive Him. Repent and believe. Put your faith and trust in who He is. Don't get caught up in these arguments, even within yourself. They only distract from the mission.

The Garden of Eden: God's Heart

Romans 5 describes God's heart for the lost. Jesus was the visible expression of the image of God. The seed—what God is like—was revealed by Christ. We know God is a sending God, a missionary God. He sent His only Son that whoever believes in Him should not perish but have everlasting life (John 3:16).

> *For a while, we were still weak at the right time; Christ died for the ungodly ... But God shows His love ...*
> Romans 5:6, 8 (ESV)

Whose love? God's love. The driving force is God's love for the lost—God's compassion. God's heart is revealed to us in the scripture; it's revealed to us in His behavior and attitude in the Garden toward Adam. As we work through these passages, I believe you will see a clearer picture of God's love for sinners, including us, and how God ministered to us while we were dead in our trespasses and sin, according to Ephesians 2:1. He came to us. God seeks the sinner. He saves the sinner, and God calls the sinner. "God showed His love toward us in that when we were still sinners, Christ died for us (Romans 5:8). Since, therefore, we have now been justified by His blood, much more we shall be saved by Him from the wrath of God." "For if while we were His enemies we were reconciled to God by the death of His Son, much more now that we are reconciled shall we be saved by His life" (Ephesians 2:5ff). God's love and pursuit of His creation are seen clearly in the Bible.

Why does He do this? Because He is a reconciling God. He's into reconciliation—the renewing and restoring of that which was lost. God desires to repair the broken fellowship and intimacy with us that He once had with Adam in the Garden.

> *And the man and his wife were both naked, and they were not ashamed.*
> Genesis 2:25

What does that mean? Why is it significant? It means that God never intended for man and woman to know what shame was. Another word for shame is "guilt" or "embarrassment." This same guilt and embarrassment they were experiencing could not have been towards the animals, and there weren't any other people around either. The shame they were experiencing was expressed toward God and God alone. They felt guilty and ashamed before God Himself. For the first time, they were experiencing something God did not create for them to experience. Here they are, full of embarrassment and guilt.

Shame and guilt are still some of Satan's top weapons. They affect us physiologically, emotionally, and spiritually; they interrupt people's lives. What percentage of our nation's population is on medication because of mental stress? Man can identify the problem, but the best we can do is put a

Band-Aid on it. We can't solve the sin problem. It's a God thing, not a man thing. It's a separation issue that requires reconciliation between man and God. Only God can fix it.

> *And they heard the sound of the Lord God walking in the garden in the cool of the day, and the man and his wife hid themselves from the presence of the Lord God among the trees in the garden. But the Lord had called the man and said, "Where are you?"*
>
> Genesis 3:8-9

These are some of the most powerful words from God to man. He wasn't asking for their geographical location. God was not confused. Looking at this in the original language, God is asking, "Adam, what have you done?" Remember, this was the seventh day of creation. What was God doing on the seventh day? He was resting. God got up from His rest to pursue Adam and Eve on His day of rest.

Do we have this same heart? The Pharisees didn't do anything on the Sabbath. They wouldn't touch a sinner. They avoided being defiled because they knew ceremonial cleansing would be required as a result. The Sabbath was their holy day. They wouldn't go out of their way to pick up a sinner and bring him into a church. But God is asking Adam, "Where are you?" God arose from His rest. He had heard something strange in creation. There was a rumble in the jungle, and He got up from His rest to see about it. Something wasn't right. God was resting, but His calm was interrupted. He went to the now-defiled Adam and Eve, the created beings He loved and fellowshipped with.

When was the Lamb slain? Before the foundations of the world were created (Revelation 13:8). Why didn't God stop Adam from sinning? Has anyone ever asked you that question when you are evangelizing? God could have stopped it, but He was resting. He had a plan in place. Why didn't God stop Adam from sinning is the wrong question. The real question is, "If we are so wicked, why should God die for us?" If we're such vile sinners, why would God die for us? The question of our guilt is the right question.

God calls out and says, "Adam, where are you?" God is pursuing Adam. The love of God is causing Him to get up from His rest and chase man. God is love. God's nature is to reconcile Himself to His creation which He loves and to whom He was intimately related. "Adam, where are you? What have you done, Adam?" Why is He asking Adam this? He wants the man to admit his problem. He wants him to come clean and not try fixing what he can't fix. God rose from His rest to seek out His creation.

Adam was driven out of the Garden by God in Genesis 3:24. This reminds me of the story of the two prodigal sons in Luke 15. One left home and came back, and the other never left home. There are two stories in Luke 15: the prodigal God, which you don't hear much about, and the prodigal sons. A couple of things are going on in this story Jesus is telling. Adam was driven from the Garden. Do you know what God felt like when He put the man out of the Garden? We know His heart. Do you think He was angry? Was He broken? Don't you think the pain in God's heart was immense? "Adam, you have to go. You cannot stay here." It did not have to be this way. The human will to choose is powerful.

Isn't that just like the father with his son in Luke 15? "You can't stay here; you have to go. I love you. This isn't what I intended for you." "Adam, this shame, this guilt isn't what I had planned for you, but now you have to go. You will have to learn a different way, Adam. You need to go around the mountain to work by the sweat of your brow. This is not what I had for you! It's not what I created you for. But I love you and desire to be with you forever."

A few chapters later, following Cain's committing the first murder, God put a mark on his head so no one would touch him. God puts a mark on the heads of sinners around you and me. It's a mark of mercy that should be a bullseye for you and me to see so we can bring them the Gospel. Look for the mark. Get beyond the fog of the day to see the souls desperately in need of being reconciled to God. Get your feet off the shore. Say, "Lord, here I am. Get me to the other side so I can learn what You have for me. There's a sound—a neighbor. Lord, teach me to labor in the vineyard, day and night, without ceasing." Where do I start? Start with prayer.

God pursued Adam. God is still pursuing the lost today. But man is still hiding in the darkness. God comes as the source of light and love because that is Who He is—He is love. Picture it like this: "Adam, maybe you're trying to hide from Me. Adam, maybe you don't want to depend on Me anymore and have a relationship with Me, but Adam, just because you don't want a relationship with Me doesn't mean I want to live without you. I love you. I want to be in a relationship with you!" God says.

God is a sending God. God, the Father, sent His only Son, Jesus. Jesus sent the Spirit to us to live in us. It's all God's work. It's all God's purpose. He came to Adam; He arose from His rest and asked, "Where are you?"

WHY NOT YOU?

God's love and compassion are seen in His love toward sinners (Genesis 3:9). God's love is seen in His pursuit of Adam. God's love is demonstrated to all sinners in John 3:16: "For God so loved [you and me] …" Jesus is the visible expressed image of God's love (Colossians 1:15).

In Luke 4, Jesus revealed more of God's heart for the lost when He quoted Isaiah 61 at the inauguration of His ministry. He read from the scroll in the synagogue, saying, "The Spirit of the Lord is upon me." Then He told the people exactly why the Spirit had come on Him—to preach the Gospel. Jesus came to preach liberty, to set captives free. He specifically tells us why He was sent and what God's power within Him would accomplish. All authority in heaven and earth has been given to Jesus (Matthew 28). He who has all power and authority abides in us! Let Him get your feet off the shore. Remember, "You can never cross the ocean unless you have the courage to lose sight of the shore." Are you willing to go beyond what you know today and let God use you? Are you willing to say, "Here I am. Send me!" (Isaiah 6:8), or are you going to hide behind the fog and not realize that another half a mile would have gotten you to shore? Hidden in the fog is the reality that sharing the Gospel one more time could have been someone's day of salvation.

> *And I sought for a man among them, that should make up the hedge, and stand in the gap before me for the land, that I should not destroy it:*
> but I found none.
>
> Ezekiel 22:30

God is pursuing the lost and calling the saved. Will you respond in obedience? Will God find someone in your church to "stand in the gap?" Will God find you answering His request to be the tool in His hand that transforms your community?

> *How think ye? If a man has a hundred sheep, and one of them be gone astray, doth he not leave the ninety-and-nine, and goeth into the mountains, and seeketh that which is gone astray?*
>
> Matthew 18:12

God's heart for the lost compels Him to seek those who have gone astray. He searched for all of us at one time or another. His concern for you and me is so great that He will leave the sheep flock to find and return the one who has wandered off. This is a perfect picture of God's heart for the lost.

When Jesus set out to confront the demoniac, it was not convenient. He crossed a large lake and headed northeast. Jesus journeyed far for that one soul. No one else could help him. This story is recorded to help us see that the demonized man represents you and me. We were as bound by our chains of sin as the demoniac was. That blind man, Bartimaeus, represents you and me in the depths of our sin apart from God. We were as blind as blind Bartimaeus, dead in our trespasses and sins (Ephesians 2:1). Aren't you glad He came for the one—for you and for me?

For the Son of man is come to seek and to save that which was lost.
Luke 19:10

God saves the sinner. Salvation is the primary goal of Biblical evangelism. Jesus has done everything that needs to be done to change the life of every human being who has or ever will live on this planet. His goal was to find and rescue those who cannot save themselves. "Salvation" means "to heal, restore, keep safe, and rescue from danger." Jesus came to restore people and creation to health. God is a restoring God, driven by His love for people. He sent His son to pay the debt of sin for all mankind.

God saves sinners. He also calls the sinner. He calls them not in order to discover where they are; He already knows. God calls sinners so that they will know where they are. The discovery of their distance from God should cause sinners to turn and be reconciled to God. God calls in a loud voice, inviting all who will believe to trust in Him. Sin is a danger to all, and God has made a way of rescue so that none need perish. When Jesus died on the cross, He dealt with sin. He rendered sin powerless to harm any of His own. When He rose from the dead, He disarmed death. Death was the power of sin, and Christ destroyed them both. They no longer have power over the lives of anyone in Christ. God calls sinners to repent and follow Him.

It's time to see through the fog and make the final effort to reach our goal. It's time to get off the shore and into the boat so that we can go beyond the horizon to the other side. It's time to let Father use us. The heart of God for the lost is described in the fourfold goal of Biblical evangelism. The first and primary goal is salvation. Jesus came to seek the lost and to save them. We are called to continue His work on earth under the guidance of His

Holy Spirit. The second goal of Biblical evangelism is discipleship. God sent the Spirit to adopt us as sons and daughters. He longs for mature children who will labor with Him to reap the harvest of souls He has prepared for us to reach. The next step of Biblical evangelism is service. Involvement in active ministry to others in your church and community is the ultimate goal of being saved. The fourth goal is training new believers to be used by the Lord of the Harvest, for them to be disciple-ers themselves. The course of evangelism is complete when the disciple becomes a disciple-er. God is calling His children to become fathers and mothers to disciple and raise mature followers of Jesus Christ. God's heart for the lost motivates Him to pursue man. His heart becomes our heart through the work of the Holy Spirit. Let the Spirit put the heart of God in you and watch what God will do with you. "Now abides faith, hope, and love. The greatest of these is love." Let the love of God fill you until it overflows in compassion for others.

A Compassionate Heart

God has a heart for the lost. How can we develop a heart of compassion for the lost? How can we grow in Christ's love for others? How can Jesus manifest Himself through us to reach those around us on a daily basis?

The most impactful concept of the past 2,000 years has been the expression of Christ's compassion through His people. It's what drew you and me and millions of others to become followers of Jesus Christ. Along with hardships, nothing turns our hearts to God more than the realization of Christ's dying for our sins on the cross. It reduces us to nothing. When we see the reality of our sin compared to the fact that Christ became sin for us, we cannot help but see how amazing His love is. When we learn that we can be restored and our lives renewed, yielding to His call is the only proper response.

The most effective, visible display of God's love is Christ's crucifixion on the cross. More than any other attribute of God, His compassion moves us. His compassion constitutes His kindness.

A Maasai tribesman was converted to follow Jesus by a missionary. The Maasai are a large East African tribe with a rich culture and traditions. This young man had a few discussions with the missionary and eventually accepted Jesus as his personal Savior. Immediately, he became a different man. He went back to his tribe with a desire to tell them what had happened to him. He was very excited to take this message back to his people. He could not wait to share how he was born again. He desired to tell his tribe how God forgave him and gave him a new life. He was sure all of his people would receive this new message, but to his dismay, everyone he told got angry with him. The men held him down while the women of the tribe beat him with barb-wired clubs. They left him nearly dead beside the road near his village. He called out to God, asking Him what he had done wrong. He wondered if he had not communicated well or had not represented Jesus well. Perhaps, he thought, he needed to try again and do a better job of telling them about Jesus.

He returned to his village, all bloodied, and preached to them again. The same thing happened. The men held him down while the women beat him even harder than before. It appeared to them as if he were dead, so they dumped him on the side of the road. Lying there, bleeding out, with what strength he had left in him, he got up and said to himself, "Surely they are not understanding." So, he got up and went back to his village, and sure enough, they didn't even wait for him to begin preaching. For a third time, the men held him down while the women beat him. But as the women were beating him, they suddenly began to weep. Then they stopped beating him, and all of them put their faith and trust in Jesus Christ. The entire tribe became followers of Jesus Christ. This was an act of God's compassion through a Maasai convert. He was a new believer who could not help but share what had happened to him.

This is the same compassion that you and I have experienced through Christ. This is the same compassion that declares, "While we were His enemies, He loved us. While we were whipping Him, Jesus died for us" (Romans 5). While our sins, and the sins of the whole world combined, were laid on the crucified Christ, He declared and asked the Father to forgive them.

Evangelizing in the Vernacular

The difference between evangelizing and witnessing is important to repeat here. Witnessing is what we do. Evangelism is the proclamation of the Good News or what we say. When we evangelize, we proclaim the Good News, and we need to speak in everyday language so all can understand. If we are going to be effective, our audience needs to understand us, and they need to understand the Gospel. It's not that complicated. We need to speak the way Christ did. He spoke in parables so that they would understand. He spoke to them in real-life language. He spoke Aramaic, the common tongue of their culture. I am not saying we need to be culturally relevant at the expense of being Biblical. I'm afraid in an attempt to reach our culture, we have placed an overemphasis in the church on being culturally relevant. I'm not saying disregard the culture or become so ingrained in the culture that you no longer are Biblically sound. I'm saying speak plain English. Speak in plain language so all can understand.

One time, I was preaching in Georgetown, a busy district near Washington, D.C. I hadn't been saved long; I was fresh off the streets at that time, which helped in this situation. I was preaching the Gospel with others, and one of the brothers with me, who had grown up his whole life on a farm, began talking to someone who had lived in the inner city his whole life. There was a lot of miscommunications happening because one person was speaking inner-city "Ebonics," and the brother was sharing the Gospel in King James English. The guy was very interested in hearing about Christ but was struggling to connect all of the dots simply because King James English was so foreign to him. I saw what was happening, chuckled, and stepped in to bridge the gap between the two by just coming along and reiterating what my brother was sharing with him in plain English. Evangelism is what we say, and we need to say it, so our audience understands.

The Compassion of the Good Samaritan

Luke 10 tells us the story of the Good Samaritan. It's a powerful story describing the unconditional compassion of God for people. Compassion is a language that transcends all tongues. This caring man from a shunned ethnic group, the Samaritans, demonstrated the compassion Christ was trying to get the people of His day to see. The religious leaders of the day were attempting to discredit Jesus with their legalism. They were asking Him questions that were relevant to only a religious mindset, but they were not concerned with the tragic plight of their fellow man. They wanted to be justified in their own eyes because they were controlled by their self-righteousness. The contrast between religious self-love and the compassion of God is dramatic in this simple story of one man who cared.

One day an expert in religious law stood up to test Jesus by asking Him this question: "Teacher, what should I do to inherit eternal life?"

Jesus replied, "What does the law of Moses say? How do you read it?" Jesus answered, "You must love the LORD your God with all your heart, all your soul, all your strength, and all your mind. And love your neighbor as yourself.'" "Right!" Jesus told him. "Do this, and you will live!" The man wanted to justify his actions, so he asked Jesus, "And who is my neighbor?" The expert in the law wanted to justify himself, so he had to ask the question: "Who is my neighbor?" Jesus replied with a story: "A Jewish man was traveling from Jerusalem down to Jericho, and he was attacked by bandits. They stripped him of his clothes, beat him up, and left him half dead beside the road. By chance, a priest came along. But when he saw the man lying there, he crossed to the other side of the road and passed him by. A Temple assistant (or a Levite) walked over and looked at him lying there, but he also passed by on the other side. Then a despised Samaritan came along, and when he saw the man, he felt compassion for him. Going over to him, the Samaritan soothed his wounds with olive oil and wine and bandaged them. Then he put the man on his own donkey and took him to an inn, where he took care of him. The next day he handed the innkeeper two silver coins, telling him, 'Take care of this man. If his bill runs higher than this, I'll pay you the next time I'm here.' Now, which of these three would you say was a neighbor to the man who was attacked by bandits?" Jesus asked. The man replied, "The one who showed him mercy." Then Jesus said, "Yes, now go and do the same" (Luke 10:25-29).

It was the Samaritan who felt compassion and then expressed compassion by going to the man and caring for him. This is a personal message to us. Jesus is saying, "Now, YOU go!"

A famous quote from Teddy Roosevelt that has since been popularized by John Maxwell goes like this: "Nobody cares how much you know until they know how much you care." Now, I'm not saying that you have to earn the right to become someone's best friend before you tell him about Jesus. But I am saying that sincere compassion speaks for itself. Being kind, friendly, and loving people will often naturally provide an opportunity to share the Gospel.

D.L. Moody writes of a lot of conversions that took place on the battlefield during the Civil War. He worked as a chaplain before he was an evangelist. People were dying of their wounds in the conflict. He was leading hundreds to faith in Jesus Christ as they were dying. He didn't have time to get to know them first. The common factor is always the compassion of God expressed through the Gospel.

Let's contrast our lives with the Good Samaritan. God has made us people full of compassion and love, but we need Christ in us to demonstrate it. He's given us all things that pertain to life and godliness already (2 Peter 1:3). You already have everything you need. Jesus is perfect in His compassion, faithfulness, and love. Guess where He lives when you become born again. In you! We must continually let Him express Himself in us and through us.

The New American Oxford Dictionary defines compassion as "having a sympathetic pity and concern for the sufferings or misfortunes of others." The Greek word used in the New Testament to describe the compassion of Jesus, according to Thayer's lexicon, means "to be moved with mercy and have pity."

Jesus was called a friend of sinners and sat with winebibbers. How is that reconciled with "to be a friend of the world makes you an enemy of

God?" (James 4:4). The Bible has no contradictions, but sometimes our understanding may be confused. Often, we are guilty of being like one of the Pharisees and not like the Good Samaritan. In our desire to live holy, we can become separated from our neighbors and our coworkers. We don't bring them the Gospel because we disassociate instead of associating. Association is another word for friendship. Association was what Jesus did. It's tough to share the Gospel with someone you don't talk to or speak with. But we can't disassociate and isolate from them. Isolation makes it impossible to show compassion.

I have heard about the concept of the "Jesus-smile." You just smile and give them the "Jesus-look." How does that work? I'm really curious. What about the "Jesus-smile" would cause someone to get saved? We have to proclaim the Gospel. Faith comes by hearing and hearing by the message of Jesus (Romans 10). It takes words to communicate the Gospel.

Matthew 18:27-30 instructs us to have compassion. The unforgiving servant threatened the guy who owed him two bucks. The master asks the servant, "Should you not have had compassion as I have had with you?" Ephesians 4:32 tells us to be kind, tender-hearted, and forgiving of one another, even as God in Christ has forgiven us. Should not the servant have had compassion too?

The depth of the debt we owe God for our personal sins is so immense that there's nothing we can do about it. This parable reveals the depth of the personal debt we owe God. It's not a story about another person; this is about you and me. There is a division between God and us. God forgave the servant and said, "Don't lose sight of your personal forgiveness in Christ and demonstrate your appreciation by expressing this same compassion to others."

There's no greater thing we can do than lead someone to turn to God and put his faith in Christ to receive eternal life, for that is the greatest expression of compassion. Compassion has visible attributes and expressions. God loved the world so much He gave (John 3:16). He gave. He gave me something. There was giving involved—resources, time, commitment, and availability were sacrificed. You can give without loving, but you cannot love without giving!

We're good at serving one another in our churches, called the Body of Christ, and we should be. The Bible tells us to do good to all, especially to the household of faith. John 13:35 says, "By this shall all men know that ye are my disciples if we have love one to another." But Christians who are committed to their churches, as we should be, can focus on the household of faith and forget to do good to those outside the family of God. We are called to do good to all. Why? Because God is good. When we do good to all, we're reflecting the image of God. We are showing to others what He's like. They will know we are followers of Christ by our love.

When Jesus looked over Jerusalem, He wept because His love was so deep for the people there. He was filled with compassion. God as a man in the flesh, as a human, was filled with compassion. The compassion of Christ caused Him to see people around Him as they were fainting. They listened to Him, but they were fainting. He noticed they were fainting. He had compassion. He didn't want to send them away when they were hungry. Is there any pity in you when someone comes to you and they're hungry? Do you send them away hungry? Jesus didn't send them away hungry. Jesus was filled with compassion which caused Him to see people around Him as sheep without a shepherd. When they had nothing to eat, when they were unable to pay their debt, when they could not afford a doctor, when they were diseased and sick, when they were demon-possessed and bound by Satan, and when they were in pain for losing a loved one, He had compassion for them. All those running away, like Adam rebelling and running away from God, Jesus loved them. God's response to all of these things He witnessed as a man, as a human being here in the flesh, was compassion. His life was an expression of His compassion. That's what Jesus in us still does today.

How to Develop a Heart for the Lost

Three things can help us develop a deeper heart of compassion for the lost.

The first is prayer. We must be seeking God with all our hearts. The second is an eternal vision. We must see the reality of the eternal condition of those who have received Jesus and those who reject him. Third, we need to remember God's kindness and mercy towards us and others. These three things will go a long way to developing compassion for the lost.

Let's deal with the first, prayer and seeking God. William Booth said:

"I will tell you the secret: God has had all that there was of me. There have been men with greater brains than I, even greater opportunities, but from the day I got the poor of London on my heart and caught a vision of what Jesus Christ could do with them and me on that day, I made up my mind that God should have all of

William Booth there was. And if there is anything of power in the Salvation Army, it is because God has had all the adoration of my heart, all of the power of my will, and all the influence of my life."

From the day Booth arrived to serve the poor of London, he was led by a vision. He caught a glimpse of God's heart. It didn't just happen; he didn't just stumble across it. He was seeking God. It was birthed in prayer. It was birthed out of the visible sufferings he could see around him. In his time with God, he had to answer the question, "What am I going to do?" He realized God might be able to do something with him if he was willing to go all-in with God. He caught a vision.

The role of prayer that leads to catching this vision is absolutely critical. Ephesians 6:12-13 (NLT) states:

> *For we are not fighting against flesh and blood enemies but against evil rulers and authorities of the unseen world. Against mighty powers in this dark world and against evil spirits in the heavenly places. Therefore, put on every piece of God's armor so you will be able to resist the enemy in the time of evil. Then after the battle, you will still be standing firm.*

Paul uses military terminology here. "We are not fighting against flesh and blood." This indicates it is not personal. Prayer makes it personal. It becomes personal because it reminds you and me that we are soldiers of the cross. We are ambassadors of Christ—ambassadors of the cross. When we start praying for the lost around us, it becomes personal. It's not just a doctrine that says, "We wrestle not against flesh and blood." It is personal because the Gospel has been entrusted to you and me (Ephesians 2:7). God left this earth, commanded us with the commission, and trusted that we would perpetuate it to another generation. It's personal, and it needs to be personal with each of us. We must catch the vision for the mission and declare, "That's my coworker; that's my neighborhood; that's my city; those are my friends' kids; that's my family; those are my children." It needs to be personal. When you put on the armor of God and dig into prayer, it goes from impersonal to personal.

The devil does not want you and me to take this personally because he knows we're going to put on that armor, dig in, and do something about it. John 16 gives us insight into this kind of intercessory prayer: "Until now, you have not asked. Ask, and you will receive that your joy may be full" (John 16:24).

It's exciting when you lead someone to the Lord and when one in captivity to the enemy is delivered. The angels are rejoicing when sinners repent and turn to God (Luke 15:10), but they are not the only ones rejoicing. We're rejoicing too! It's an occasion to celebrate. It comes full circle when a year after someone has been saved, he leads someone else to the Lord, and then another, and then another, etc. Look how many lives can be touched. You can't do that with money. You touch generations when you reach people for Christ. That's the greatest investment.

Intercessory prayer is when we take the lost before the Lord. Intercessory prayer is when you and I take before the Lord the same causes and purposes that He cares about. The things that are on His heart and His mind become our concerns when we pray. When we join His mission through prayer for others, we are entering into a co-laboring with Christ. Praying for the lost is simply yoking up with Christ and saying, "Lord, here am I, send me!"

The vision came first to Isaiah in Isaiah 6. He saw a vision of God, and he cried out to be sanctified, and after that sanctification, he said, "Here am I." The Lord said, "Who will go for us?" Isaiah didn't ask where, what, or how long. Isaiah's response to God's question is seen in Luke 10:2 when Jesus declares the fields are white unto harvest. He instructs, "Pray to the Lord of the harvest that He send forth more laborers." The fields have been ripe for over 2,000 years. They have always been ripe. The harvest is plentiful; the laborers are few. Don't say the doors aren't open. Prayer is battling against spirits. We go to battle against principalities and powers because it's personal. This is how revival starts. Why not let it begin with you and me? If twelve can turn the world upside down, surely, we can take our town for Christ! John 16:24 says, "You haven't done this before. Ask, using My name, and you will receive, and you will have abundant joy."

Ask! We can use His name. We will have abundant joy as a result. What do we ask for? Ask Him to give you His heart and mind. Ask Him to change your heart. "Lord, make me aware of the reality of who You are in me. Help me to get out of Your way so that You can express Your compassion through me in bringing others the Gospel." That's a good prayer. Do you think He'll answer it? If we ask anything according to His will, He hears it (1 John 5:14); it's a done deal. Can you remember a time when you prayed to be used to bring someone the Gospel, and it didn't happen? Has that ever happened to anyone? Have you ever asked God to reach a soul, and He never led you to one? I've never had that happen in my life. Maybe you've never asked. Start asking; it's not too late!

WHY NOT YOU?

Ask Him to make your heart like His. Ask for the salvation of others. Ask God to change you. Ask Him to change those around you. Pray for God to enlarge your heart and commit to the course of His commandments. Request that God change you so that others will be changed. Ask God to sanctify you. Jesus prayed in John 17 for others to be sanctified. We ask God to sanctify us so others might be sanctified, too. This is not to gain a holiness badge. It's not about rank or approval. The blood is the badge we need. We're washed in the blood. We're separated from the lost by a thin layer of blood; that's the only difference. There is nothing intrinsically good in us. Jesus is in us, and that's all we need. It is more than enough.

Ask for the salvation of those around you. First, John 5:14 says, "If we ask according to His will, He hears us." Psalm 2:8 reveals what God will give you if you ask. He promises to give us the nations. God says He'll give us the nations! That's God's heart. He is describing His heart. He says, "I'm willing to give you the nations." Are you willing to stand and intercede with Him? Are you going to join Him? What country is on your heart?

I remember when we were looking at the mission field after I got saved in 1989. I was praying about which country to go to, waiting on God to show me. I was consecrated to God. I knew I was going; I was just waiting for God to show me which country. I was praying with friends about it. God put Latin America on my heart. I dedicated my life to winning souls in Latin America. For the rest of my life, my soul is going to burn out for it. God may not call you to Latin America. We are called to grow where we're planted. It is where you live, work, and go to school today. This is your neck of the woods. God has put you in that part of the vineyard to gather that harvest together with Him.

God clearly wants us to ask. He takes delight when His children ask. Proverbs 11:30 says, "He who wins souls is wise." That's not exactly what it means, but there's a principle in it. God takes delight when we ask. James 5:16 describes prayer that is effectual. Effectual means "to be at work, operating, and effective." Oxford Dictionary defines it as "hot, burning, on fire." We need to be on fire! It means "to display an intensity." Do you get nervous when someone stares you down? I stare back at them, give them that "Jesus-smile." Maybe I'll win them over.

Developing a compassionate heart begins with prayer and seeking God. It continues with a vision of eternity. When I see Jesus, I'll behold Him. I'll be like Him; I'll be satisfied with Him. When I see Him, I live for that moment. I came just one breath away from death recently. I can't wait for that, but I'm here to take people with me. I realized for me to take people with me is one thing; for me and forty others to do it is another. We're in this together. We are in it to win souls. We're going after the salvation of people. We have a mission and a co-mission, and we have grace and anointing and power. Take hold of it! Step out! Let the Spirit use you to change lives!

Most Christian leaders would like to send their recruits to Bible college for five years. Shawn David is credited with saying, "If I could have my way, I would not send my young ministers to seminary or Bible college. I would have all of them spend five minutes in hell." That would do more than anything else to prepare them for a lifetime of compassionate ministry.

Five years of Bible college versus five minutes in hell, and this brother felt the five minutes in hell would be more effective for a lifetime of compassionate ministry. You see, without a vision (Proverbs 29:18), the people perish. Some translations say, "They cast off restraint" without a vision. Without a vision, which means a prophetic vision or revelation from God, we perish. We need the vision of the condition of their souls, their eternal condition. We need the reality of what they are facing every day. Have we lost sight of the plight of the lost? He loves us. Why do we love Him? Because He first loved us. It was His idea. It was in His heart to love you and me. Is it in my heart to love you, to prefer you, to honor you above me in every situation? Do I desire to be like Christ? Love allows us to forgive when we've been wronged or mocked. We can forgive with the love and compassion of Christ because Jesus lives in us. It's not me who lives anymore. Paul said, "But Christ who lives in me. The life I live now in the flesh, I live by the faith and trust of the Son of God who loved me, died for me, gave Himself for me" (Galatians 2:20).

Scripture says Jesus wept over Jerusalem. Do we weep? When was the last time you wept? Do you see the need? If you can see the need, you can touch the need. See the need; touch the need. Touch the need by getting involved and by looking for opportunities, praying for wisdom. See the need; touch the need. In Romans 9:2, Paul confesses he had great sorrow and unnecessary anguish on behalf of his people. Are we having great sorrow and anguish? Beloved, I'm not here to condemn you. I'm asking myself these questions. I've ebbed and flowed in the love of God. I don't want to ebb and flow. I want to go because when I go, God shows up. I don't want to ebb and flow, and I know you don't either. I know when I step out, God shows up. The Spirit went with the disciples, confirming the Word as they proclaimed it. We want to see miracles without stepping out of the boat. It doesn't work that way. Jesus is more than willing. Ask, and you will receive. It gets exciting when we go for it. Take Him at His word. Starting now, don't wait.

Paul said: "It was impressed on my mind, on my conscience by the Holy Spirit." This great sorrow and unnecessary anguish. Paul said he was "impressed in his mind and conscience. It was impressed like on a printing press. It was stamped on his mind. We need the reality of the plight of those around us— the lost, our neighbors, our coworkers. This reality needs to be impressed on our minds so that we can't stop thinking about it; it's on our minds 24/7. Believers can't lose the reality of eternal hell. If we really believe, we would be motivated by love to win others. We must repent and trust Jesus as our Savior 24/7. It motivates us. We need that vision. We need a vision of hell. We need to see the reality of it. Ephesians 2:7 says we have been entrusted with the Gospel. What are we doing with it?

Vision will direct us to lead people to Christ and pray for that wisdom. Without a vision, we will loosen our grip. The vision won't be impressed on our minds like it was on Paul's. People will fall when someone who was holding them lets go. Jesus prayed for you and me, and He still is. We get that privilege of praying for others—holding them up before God. Compassion will recognize the suffering around us and do everything possible to lead people to faith in Christ.

We begin with prayer, continue with vision, and ultimately serve with kindness. Kindness opens doors (Romans 2:4). Do we presume on the kindness of God? His kindness is meant to lead us to repentance. The loving-kindness of God leads us to repentance. He first loved us. First, Thessalonians 4:12 and Colossians 4:5 admonishes us to walk wisely and be representatives of how we walk toward outsiders. Do good to all. Luke 6:35 says God is kind to the ungrateful and evil. We are to put on compassionate hearts and act with kindness (Colossians 3:12). We put on these things by the grace of God. Holiness can be seen. Holiness is a visible attribute. Wear it with joy.

Three things can help us have a heart of compassion for the lost:

Pray for them.
Weep for them.
Be kind to them.

Will you let God put a heart of compassion for the lost in you?

The Gospel Clear and Simple

Evangelism requires the clear and simple communication of the Gospel. The RMS Titanic, a British ocean liner built in 1908 and operated by the White Star Line, sank in the North Atlantic Ocean on April 15, 1912, after striking an iceberg during her maiden voyage from South Hampton to New York City. Of the estimated 2,224 passengers and crew aboard, more than 1,500 died, making the sinking one of the deadliest of a single ship and the deadliest peacetime sinking of a super-liner or cruise ship at the time. As a modern marvel, it had all the bells and whistles of that era, including a top-of-the-line Marconi, a wireless Morse code communication system. The communication service maintained a twenty-four-hour schedule, primarily sending and receiving passenger telegrams but also handling the navigation messages, including weather reports and ice warnings. "Weather delightful" was one of the messages sent out just before the ship struck the iceberg. Passengers were sending messages to friends and family on land with notes brought to the Titanic's wireless officer, Jack Phillip, who sent them via Morse code. Following this final cheery message about the nice weather, the next message Phillip sent was direr. "Come at once, have struck a berg." The Titanic began to send distress signals while gradually taking on water but calls for help on the telegraph line took time.

Other ships kept asking for more information and confirmation of the disaster. The communication system became clogged with so many incoming and outgoing messages that the Titanic's SOS pleas were getting lost. They could not prioritize real-time urgent messages. "We are putting passengers off in small boats. Women and children in boats. Cannot last much longer. Losing power," said one of the last messages sent out. Within two hours and forty minutes, sixty-eight percent of all on board were dead. Only one-third of those on board survived. The White Star Line actually provided more lifeboat accommodations than were legally required; however, at the time, lifeboats were only intended to ferry survivors from a sinking ship to a rescuing ship. They were not intended to keep the whole population afloat or power them to shore. Had the closest ship, the SS Californian, responded to the Titanic's distress calls, the lifeboats may have been adequate to ferry the passengers to safety as planned.

Communication Has Eternal Consequences

Overconfidence in the technology of the ship fooled the captain into being less diligent than required. Lives could still have been saved if communication had been swifter and clearer. Lives were lost in this historic disaster because the message of the distress was not communicated simply and clearly.

Poor communication can lead to serious and possibly eternal consequences. Communication is very important. Had there been more effective communication—with people listening to the messages communicated—the signals might not have gotten clogged, and lives may have been saved. Only one-third of those on board The Titanic survived her sinking. The only difference between those who survived this tragedy and those who did not was that the survivors were able to get in a lifeboat. There was no Plan B for salvation that day. There was no other way to be saved or delivered from the water that day. There is no Plan B in the Gospel that we are sharing with the lost.

No alternative will save. "There is none other name under heaven given among men, whereby we must be saved" (Acts 4:12). We have to bring a sense of urgency when we are communicating the Gospel. We can't let our fear take control of us when we're sharing the message of Jesus Christ. We can't anticipate rejection; we can't let fear keep us from sharing. We must clearly and effectively share the Good News. It's a learning process. We must learn from the wisdom of the Word, the Holy Spirit in us, and even from others. We can gain from the experience of others who have been doing it longer, books we have read, and talking to others.

Evangelism is a lifestyle learned mostly by loving people and sharing with them the Gospel clearly and simply.

What is the goal of preaching the Gospel and communicating clearly? We're called to walk in the ministry God has given us. We know Scripture reveals our ministry is the ministry of reconciliation. One of the things we are trying to communicate is that God in Christ is redeeming the world to Himself (2 Corinthians 5:19). The things we want to be able to explain are simply this:

WHY NOT YOU?

1. Who is Jesus?
2. Why did Jesus die for all?
3. How does someone become right with God through Jesus?

Who and why are the questions to be answered when we share the Gospel. Why do we need Christ? Why do we need to put our faith and trust in this man who died 2,000 years ago on a cross? What's the significance of His sacrifice? What's the purpose of His life? Doesn't that sound like lunacy? "You are telling me about some dude I never met who died 2,000 years ago. You want me to trust him? He can save me from hell; Jesus can reconcile me to God?" Eternal life—being born again—is more than a destination. It's more than a place we are going. It's not a church building but a Person, God. It's eternal life; it is Christ in us, the hope of glory. It's not Christ's dying for us just so we can go to heaven: that's a simple understanding of the Gospel, but the most important part. The foremost benefit of believing and becoming a Christian is to avoid the judgment of eternal hell and being in heaven for all eternity with God. We need to be able to explain what sin is and why it has condemned mankind.

Our culture's reference to sin has shifted in the past decades. In my early days as a Christian, if I mentioned sin, there was a reference point most could connect with because there was more of a Judeo-Christian influence in our culture thirty years ago. Today in our discussions, many people don't understand what sin is. We need to be able to explain what sin is.

Mark 7:14–23 says that sin comes from the heart. Sins are the things that proceed out of the heart. Sin is what comes naturally to someone who does not believe in and receive Jesus Christ. We can't miscommunicate the Gospel and judge people as rejecting God afterward. We can't condemn them for our shortcomings. That would be a disservice. We can't hold someone accountable for what he didn't understand. We can't say, "Aw, to hell with them. They just rejected God." They didn't understand a lick of what we said when we were speaking King James English to them for the last twenty minutes. They were politely nodding their heads, trying not to offend us. I've seen this happen. I've done it before. I'm not saying people aren't going to reject God. Most people like the forgiveness part of Jesus, but not the lordship, surrendering to His will part. Rejection of God is a consequence of sin. Sin rejects God, but that's not what we're talking about. It's critical we, with simplicity and clarity, are able to explain the Gospel.

We can learn each time we share. We need to ask, "How can I be more effective, Lord?" Don't be under condemnation. Don't be self-analytical. Self-analysis creates spiritual paralysis. Even if we did a bad job of sharing the Gospel, the Lord takes delight when we step out in faith to honor Him in obedience. What does the most damage is a hypocritical life, living in sin like the world yet proclaiming Jesus as Lord. If that is you, simply repent and let God have every part of your life. We are not trying to convince them with the wisdom of men. We're not using enticing words in the power of man; we're going in the power of the Holy Ghost (1 Corinthians 2:4). God has something to say in you and through you. We're stepping out in faith, obedience, and love for our Father because we want to see His name glorified on the earth. Through us, He will touch broken lives just like He touched you and me.

To be successful in evangelizing or sharing the Gospel, we need to:

+ Remind ourselves how Christ gave His life for every one of us. Preach the Gospel to ourselves.
+ Learn to use the Scriptures effectively.
+ Be able to communicate the Gospel with simple clarity in the hearer's language.

Preach the Gospel to Yourself

The number one factor that will make us effective when evangelizing or sharing the Gospel is the personal reminder of how Christ has redeemed and saved us. Another way of saying it is: "Preach the Gospel to yourself every day!" Why accept Jesus? What did Jesus do? How did I become right with God? These are some things we need to remind ourselves of every day. Romans 12:1 is the call to offer ourselves as "living sacrifices." How do I present my body as a living sacrifice? Paul says: "I appeal to you; therefore, brothers, by the mercies of God to present your bodies as a living sacrifice holy and acceptable to God, which is our spiritual worship." If we are going to be effective in our evangelism. We must pursue personal holiness. Evangelism is an expression of God's holiness working in and through our lives. We don't often think of the pursuit of holiness and knowing God as key aspects of evangelism. Paul very clearly pleads by the mercies of God that we present ourselves as living sacrifices. We walk this out, remembering the mercies of God. Mercy is one of God's major attributes. "But of him are ye in Christ Jesus, who of God is made unto us wisdom, and righteousness, and sanctification, and redemption" (1 Corinthians 1:30). Salvation and sanctification are accomplished through Christ's redemptive work of grace on the cross. The Holy Spirit continually works that promise through our lives to make us more like Christ in our character and the choices we make to cooperate (2 Corinthians 3:18).

We are reminded of His kindness and His love and compassion toward the lost. His mercies are another attribute of the character of God. As we meditate on God's mercies in our lives, we become more like Him as He reveals Himself to us. Where would we be without God today? If God did not become a man and live among us, become a Savior, and even become sin for our sin, where would we be today? What would our lives be like? Where would our families be? What would our children's lives be like? If we have walked with God for even a short while, we have many amazing testimonies of God's grace working in our lives. We could spend hours reciting stories of God's mercy in our lives.

You can never exhaust your understanding of the Gospel. That doesn't mean stop trying. Never stop trying to understand the Gospel. The Scriptures tell us to grow in the grace and knowledge of our Lord (2 Peter 3:18). Pursue an understanding of the Gospel. When we get the Gospel right, we understand God right. We understand God because it all ties into His attributes—who God is and what He's like.

How do we preach the Gospel to ourselves? We preach the Gospel to ourselves by reminding ourselves of God's mercies that are new every morning. I think they're new every second. We need His mercies. Meditate on the mercies of God. Paul says this will motivate us to walk out holiness. The command to go into all the world and preach the Gospel is based on this command. We will never exhaust our understanding of the Gospel; it will lead us to appreciate His mercy more and more. The reality of our righteousness and sanctification purchased by Christ's blood will deepen our love and affection for the cross, for Christ, and for His resurrection. Such contemplation will produce in us zeal to preach the Gospel. It creates the motivation to share the Gospel. Because we are full of joy, thinking about how God worked such great a salvation in our lives, we won't stop thinking about it. The more I understand the provisions of God's salvation for me personally, the more I understand what He has done for others around me and how He wants to touch them.

One of the questions we must revisit when preaching the Gospel to ourselves is: Why Jesus? Why did Christ become sin for our sin? Why did He come as the Savior of the world? There are some straightforward scriptures that answer this, and they begin the discussion with sin as the catalyst. Sin separated Adam from God. Sin separates us from God. We will look at Adam's "federal headship"—because Adam sinned, we all sinned in him. It's a theological term I'll mention so you know what it is. Sin is a disease of the soul, mind, and body. Isaiah 1:5-6 gives us some very clear insight into what this disease looks like. This disease is sin. What is sin? Why did Jesus come and have to die? He did so because there was a sin problem that separated mankind from God.

> *Why do you continue to invite punishment? Must you rebel forever? Your head is injured, your heart is sick, you are battered from head to foot covered with bruises, welts, and infected wounds without any soothing ointments or bandages.*
>
> Isaiah 1:5-6

We see here in Isaiah that, firstly, sin affects the head. That means the thoughts of man are altogether evil. Sin affects the thinking of man. It involves our thought life. It describes our thoughts apart from the grace of God.

Secondly, He mentions the heart. Our hearts are sick. The heart is the seat of the emotions. Apart from God, we have the wrong emotions towards a lot of things. Most of us don't have to go back too far to remember how wrong our thinking about God and Christ was before we got saved. Sin affects our hearts and the emotions we have toward one another, toward God, and toward life.

Third, and in addition to the head and heart, it also says we were "battered from head to foot." The writer is describing our feet, our means of locomotion. Action happens through movement by our feet. The prophet is revealing something significant here. Sin is a disease of the soul affecting thoughts, emotions, and actions. We see it all around the world; we see it in our neighborhoods. We see it in life around us. We saw it in our lives before Jesus. We see the temptation to go back to when we're not relying on the Holy Spirit in us. Where sin abounds, His grace does much more abound.

Sin is a disease of the soul. It is also a rejection of God. It's keeping for ourselves the place that belongs to God in our minds, emotions, and will. Sin is rejection of God. Sin is also disobedience to God, either by doing what He has forbidden us to do or by failing to do what He has commanded us to do. Christ lived the life I should have lived. God became a man in Jesus Christ. He lived a life we should have lived, and He died the death we should have died. We have to be able to clearly communicate what sin is and how it affects people because so many people don't understand it. We must be able to communicate it in today's common language. If we must use religious terms, we must also break down the message so anyone can understand. Most people don't know what substitutionary atonement, redemption, or propitiation are. You have to break down the Gospel into common everyday language.

The fruit and character of a good communicator or preacher is he can communicate the message to the simplest among us so even a child can understand. We want simplicity. It's not about ego. Many intellectuals become egotistical about their knowledge; they don't want to sound simple. Jesus was effective as a communicator because He talked simply. He was all-knowing, yet the intellectual thinks He didn't know very much because Jesus didn't have a degree. He was the Creator of all heaven and earth standing in front of them, but they thought they were smarter than He was. He was willing to reduce Himself to a man to meet the needs of the people by communicating the Gospel simply. We must become like that.

Sin is turning away from God and the purpose He made us for. Isaiah 53 says we have all turned to our own ways. We are missing the mark and falling short. Romans 3:23 states that everyone has sinned and fallen short of God's glorious standard. God, in His grace, freely makes us right in His sight. He did this through Christ Jesus when He freed us from the penalty of sin. God presented Jesus as the sacrifice for sin. People are made right with God when they stop trusting in their efforts to become right with God and believe that Jesus sacrificed His life, shedding His blood for them. This sacrifice shows that God was fair when He held back and did not punish those who sinned in past times.

Romans 6:23 declares the wages of sin but also reveals a gift. It tells us that the wages of sin are death. Most preachers stop there and never get to the second part of that verse. Most are bent on making sure people know they are going to die and go to hell. Often, they forget to tell them about the free gift. In our discussion of the Gospel, we're not going to talk just about sin. We describe why Jesus' death was necessary. Jesus had to come to earth as a man because there was a sin problem that separated mankind from God. Being reconciled to God, knowing God, walking with God, living for His purposes is why Jesus came. He came because sin came.

We described sin as a disease of the soul; it is the rejection of God demonstrated by disobedience to God and a turning away from Him and

His purpose. It means "missing the mark." Sin means missing the bullseyes like the arrows that miss the target. Falling short is like what would happen if I attempted to throw a rock from Virginia to Wisconsin. One throw might send that rock a long way, and another throw might not send it quite as far. But the distance doesn't matter because both of us are going to come up short. The natural mind can understand that. When we show someone the scripture in Romans 3 that explains why we're all sinners and that we all fall short of God's standard, we have to be able to communicate this truth. People need analogies to help them understand. The natural mind cannot receive the things of God. We are relying on the wisdom of the Holy Spirit, but we must be able to explain to people what sin is. You can. You know what it is. You have been set free from its power. The wages of sin is death. What are wages? Wages are things you earn from doing a job. If I paid you fifty dollars for mowing my yard, you earned a payment—a wage.

Dr. Larry Moyer of EvanTell uses an excellent simple presentation of good news/bad news that I've ever seen. I'm not opposed to methodology in approach, especially when approaching total strangers. But the only training and method you see emphasized in the Bible is to love people and help move them closer to personal faith in Jesus. The Holy Spirit is responsible for the rest of it. Love them and pray with them whenever possible. Most successful evangelists have a method. They have some systematic approaches they use to engage people with the Gospel. Whether they received it by revelation from the third heaven while praying or learned it from another person, methods can help overcome our fears.

We read about men like D.L. Moody, Billy Graham, and other evangelists. Approaching a stranger on the street is very different than talking to a coworker or neighbor. The message we're sharing is not different, and the need to be clear and simple is not different, but the relationship is different. It's very important that we have a good opening statement. I started this chapter with an opening statement. I started with a tragedy, an illustration of the effects of bad communication and why we need to have good communication. When we approach a stranger, we need an icebreaker. You can't just roll up on somebody. Dr. Moyer has one of the best opening statements I've heard. He begins with, "Has anyone shown you in the Bible how you can be certain that you are going to heaven?" "If you died today, do you know where you will spend eternity?" is another of my favorites. According to his testimony of forty years, Dr. Moyer has had only four or five people tell him yes. Most tell him no. He follows up with, "Can I show you?" When you're rolling up on a stranger, starting with the Good News is a little more inviting than starting with the bad news. We're not trusting in methodology, but there is wisdom we can glean from each other on how to approach strangers, especially today. People can be on edge when a stranger approaches, so we need to approach them properly and kindly.

Be sensitive to where they are. Maybe be open to listen for a little while. You may want to get through the whole Bible, but instead, listen, listen, and listen! Here is an extreme example of a negative approach I witnessed one day. I was walking around a corner, and there was a guy walking ahead of me. Someone pulled up next to him in a car, rolled down the window, and called to him, "Psst! Come here!" I thought I recognized the man in the car. The guy on the sidewalk must have been wondering what was happening. "This is not the way to evangelize," I thought. The guy on the sidewalk began to get mad, thinking he was being stalked, but the guy in the car was not picking up on the pedestrian's aggravation. Things were getting worse. He continued to call the stranger over to his car. When the guy on the sidewalk began to look like he had reached the point where he was about to deliver a beatdown, I walked up to the guy in the car and said, "Hey, nice to see you. This guy is ticked; you might want to back off a little bit." The guy in the car was determined to let this man know he was doomed to hell, but his approach was not working. Don't forget to share the gift. Eternal life is a gift. Begin with the Good News.

We also need to remember what Jesus did. What do we need to communicate? We're preaching the Gospel to ourselves. We're reminding ourselves of the sin we've been delivered from. We're remembering how God in Christ delivered you and me. The message doesn't stop with preaching on sin and its effects. There's a remedy. Remember, we have good news! The answer to all the world's problems is still restoration with God. We are sent to the whole world to tell of God's love and His desire to save everyone. We are to preach what provisions He made to save the world. This is the Good News of the Gospel. We get to tell of the love of God the Father, the sacrifice of Christ the Son, and the transforming power of the Holy Spirit. God loves everyone everywhere and wants to save all. John 3:16 is a classic verse for all of us.

> *For this is how God loved the world, He gave His one and only Son so that everyone who believes in Him will not perish but have eternal life. God sent His Son into the world not to judge the world but to save the world through Him. There is no judgment against anyone who believes*

in Him. But anyone who does not believe in Him has already been judged for not believing in God's one and only Son.

John 3:16-18

My point is that we gain understanding by believing, relying on, and trusting in Christ. As I sit in a chair, I assume it will hold my weight. I am trusting the chair to allow me to sit comfortably. The word "pistis" in Greek means "to believe, trust, rely on, adhere to, or cling to." When I sit in a chair, I am believing it will hold me.

Jesus said, "He who has My word and believes in Him who sent Me has everlasting life and shall not come into judgment" (John 5:24). We are saved by the Gospel, but often we get our sanctification signals crossed in the process. There is no judgment against anyone who believes in Him, but that's not speaking of our performance. We are eternally secure if we continue to believe. It's important to understand the assurance of our salvation. That's one of the things we want to get into the mind of a believer. John 5:24 is a great verse to memorize soon after we're born again.

"The Lord isn't slow about His promises as some people think" (2 Peter 3:9). This reveals something important that often gets overlooked. The Lord isn't slow about His promises. Peter is talking about the coming of the Lord and the time of His coming. The context here is the return of the Lord. God may appear to move slowly because He does not want anyone to be destroyed. The King James Version says God seems to be slow so that all may come to repentance. He does not want anyone to be destroyed. Rejecting God and staying in sin ends in destruction. God wants everyone to repent. He doesn't want anyone to be destroyed. This means everyone is a candidate to hear the Gospel. That's God's heart! You may say, "But I need a word. I need a word from God." You just got a word! I'm not talking about not believing God for specifics or being Spirit-led. I'm bringing the balance that the Word has revealed to us God's heart in the matter, and when you ask anything according to His will, He hears us.

Let's stay in 2 Peter 3 because verse 15 gives us more insight, and remember, our Lord's patience gives people time to be saved. His motive is revealed. One reason Christ hasn't returned yet is that God wants more people to be saved. There will be a time when God says, "I'm done with the harvest; I'm done." See what our beloved Peter wrote: "And remember, Our Lord's patience gives people time to be saved" (2 Peter 3:15, NLT). One translation says this "helps you." The patience of God helps you and me to be busy with His heart and His business. We are working together with Christ. We are co-laborers in God's vineyard. He is the Lord of the harvest. When the last one hears, Jesus' return will happen. Patience doesn't mean man's resistance will always be tolerated. There is a day coming when He will say, "Enough, time to come home."

Ezekiel 33 relates, "He takes no pleasure in the death of the wicked." 1 Timothy, chapter 2, verses three through six, tell us that God wants all people to be saved. How many? All! All around you and me, everywhere we go, are candidates for receiving the Gospel. Everyone, everywhere, every day. God loves everyone and wants all to be saved. This is the heart of God. He loves every one of them, even that person who was mean to you. He loves all of them.

Jesus became, in salvation, our Substitute, our Mediator, our Liberator, and our Lord. The Gospel has the power to save (Romans 1:16). When the Holy Spirit works in the life of a sinner, He helps him to repent and believe in Christ as his personal Savior and Lord. We call this "conversion." Conversion occurs when a sinner completely surrenders his whole being to God. The sinner's part is to repent and believe. It requires a change of direction, a change of attitude, and a change of mind. The Spirit convicts and helps to change the sinner who completely surrenders his life to God. This is the Holy Spirit's ministry. God's part is to convict of sin, righteousness, and unbelief. The sinner's part is to repent, believe, and surrender. Repent and belief are synonymous. Forgiveness was made available through the death of Christ, and reconciliation happens when a person repents. The Bible says both need to happen. They happen simultaneously when the Spirit is at work. One cannot be separated from the other. They are two sides of the same coin.

> *Anyone who belongs to Christ becomes a new person. The old life is gone. A new life has begun, and all of this is a gift from God. Who brought us back to Himself through Christ. And God has given us this task—God gave us this ministry of reconciliation.*
> 2 Corinthians 5:17–18

Our task, honor, and privilege are the ministry of reconciling people to Him. Psalms 126 says that those who sow in tears will come back rejoicing, bringing their sheaves with them. This is intercession. God was in Christ, reconciling the world to Himself and reconciling us to Himself. He is no longer counting our sins against us. He gave us this wonderful message of reconciliation, so we are Christ's ambassadors. Christ is making His appeal through us. Are we allowing Him to use us? Are we going? Are we making this appeal to our neighbors and loved ones? We speak for Christ when we plead, "Come back to God." For God made Christ, who never sinned, to be the offering for our sin so that we could be made right with God through Christ.

Why Jesus? Because we need a savior. Because He alone can reconcile us. He alone is the mediator, the liberator, the Lord, the substitute. These are all provisions of salvation and reconciliation. These are words that we should familiarize ourselves with because they are in the Scriptures.

Let's review:

- To become effective in our evangelism, we must share the Gospel and communicate it simply with clarity. One of the things that motivates us to do that is preaching the Gospel to ourselves.
- Asking ourselves, "Why Jesus?" Remembering why Jesus died and sin has been dealt with on the cross with His blood.
- Reminding ourselves what Jesus did. He became sin for our sin.
- Rehearsing how to tell others to receive Christ as personal Lord and Savior.

Romans 3 says, "But now, God has shown us a way to be made right with Him without keeping the requirements of the law." God has shown us a way to be right with Him! We are made right with Him by placing our faith in Jesus Christ. We stay right with God the same way. This is true for everyone who believes, no matter who he is. For everyone has sinned and fallen short of God's glory. Yet God, in His grace, freely makes us right in His sight. He did this through Jesus Christ when He freed us from the penalty of our sins. The second vital step in becoming successful in preaching the Gospel is using the Scriptures to present the Gospel clearly and with simplicity. The Scriptures are the most powerful and underutilized tool in evangelism. The presentation of the Gospel is much more powerful if I can show you in the Bible. For example, if we're discussing why Jesus is necessary, I may turn to Romans 3:23 and ask you to read it. Dr. Moyer's opening statements can be useful here: "Has anyone shown you in the Bible how you can be assured you're going to have eternal life and go to heaven? I'm going to show you you're a sinner first. I'm not going to have you read the whole Bible; I'll just share a few passages with you."

Faith comes by hearing (Romans 10:17). Hearing the Word of God is a real catalyst for faith to rise in them. No one is going to come unless the Holy Spirit is drawing him. Does the Holy Spirit want to draw them? Of course! Romans 1:16 declares the power of the Gospel. Get their eyes on the Scriptures. It does not matter if they are Catholic, Muslim, or whatever. It does not matter who they are. You do not need a degree in apologetics. You do not need to be a creation scientist. You need to get their eyes on the Scriptures because faith comes by hearing, and the Gospel is the power. The Word is alive. Get them to read the Bible. Let them see it with their own eyes. In King James language? No, in common everyday language like Jesus did it. It's going to be difficult enough for them to understand. They may not understand a lot of the words. They have a lot opposing their minds at that moment. Both the devil and their natural mind resist the things of God.

We must use wisdom and communicate with clarity and simplicity. That can be done with your phone on a Bible app. You can have a simple translation on your phone and let them read it. "Well, I don't know if that is an authorized translation because in one part of this Gospel or one part of 1 John, they left out three verses." They aren't going to be reading those three verses. It's OK. "Well, that means I'm endorsing that translation." Look, we're not trying to win a fight over the best translation; we're trying to win souls. We're trying to reach souls for Jesus. Yes, of course, doctrine is important. Use wisdom. Are you going to get hung up on translations, or are you going to become effective in communicating the Gospel? Which objective are you trying to reach? What's your goal?

Here are some Bible verses concerning the use of Scripture:

> *For as the rain and snow come down from heaven and do not return there but water the earth, making it bring forth and sprout giving seed to the sower, so shall my word be that goes out from my mouth it shall not return to me empty. But it shall accomplish that which I purpose and shall succeed it the thing I sent it to do. The Word produces and does what God intends it to do. God looks after His Word. I love what Jesus said. Jesus said these testify of Me.*
>
> Isaiah 55:10-11

The Word produces and does what God intends it to do. God looks after His Word. I love what Jesus said. Jesus said these testify of Him! See what he says in the Gospel of John:

> *You search the Scriptures because you think they give you eternal life. But the Scriptures point to Me.*
>
> John 5:39

The Scriptures point to Jesus. Who are you trying to point people to? Jesus. Why wouldn't we use the Scriptures? What does that mean? Can you do a Bible study with unsaved people? What are you studying? The Gospel. Read this. Read that. Anyone who is interested is obviously being drawn. The devil's not leading them, and their flesh cannot seek the Lord. There is none righteous; there is none that seek after God. Sow the Word, have confidence in the Word. It's alive and powerful. The Word will draw them. The Bible talks about world events. The Bible talks about how to raise your children. The Bible talks about finances. The Bible talks about every aspect of our lives. Use it. Bring it into the equation as much as you can. Psalm 119 says the Word is a lamp and guide. Obey it in every part of your life.

Luke 24: 25-27 reveals to us that Jesus used the Scriptures. Beginning with Moses and the prophets, Jesus interpreted the Scriptures in the things concerning Himself. Jesus used the Old Testament prophecies about Messiah— about Himself. He used the Scriptures to help the Jews connect the dots. "These things testify of me," He said. Jesus used the Bible for His evangelism, helping the natural minds understand the things of God. He brought people to where faith moved through the Word. The Bible says, "All Scripture is God-breathed, used for reproof, teaching, training in righteousness" (2 Timothy 3:14-17). These are written so you may believe that Jesus is the Christ. You are trying to point people to Jesus. In John 20:31, He said if He was lifted up, He would draw all people to Him. Lift Him up! Point to them to Jesus.

The third vital ingredient for successful evangelism is effective communication. There are various methods, all focusing on clear communication and type of approach. First Corinthians 15:2-4 is a beautiful summary of the Gospel and salvation. Preaching the Gospel to ourselves, using the Scriptures to evangelize the lost, and communicating the Gospel with simple clarity will help make us more effective in leading others to put their faith in Christ for salvation. Don't let fear stop you. It's the number one thing that stops people from evangelizing. Be clear and simple. Let God use you!

Going in Power

Our Gospel came to you not only in word but also in power.
In the Holy Spirit and with full conviction,
you know what kind of men we prove to be among you.
1 Thessalonians 1:5

Apostle Paul is our example of how to evangelize. He provides the ideal picture of how we want to bring the Gospel. We need words to preach the Gospel, but only the Holy Spirit can illuminate people's minds and hearts to receive. Seeing the Holy Spirit accompany the words we use to preach the Gospel is what it means to go in power. Going in power takes all the pressure off you and me because it's the Holy Spirit's ministry that brings full conviction and salvation, not our efforts and skill.

In this chapter, we're going to look at three aspects of going in power. The first is programs versus prayer. The second is the understanding that to be ambassadors of reconciliation, we need to be intentional. Our third point is going with healing hands, expecting to see God's power move through us. Sharing the Gospel is a cosmic battle in the spiritual realm. Going in power means doing what Jesus did, and at almost every turn, He applied healing hands and cast out demons. These were primary components of His earthly ministry.

In Acts 4, verses 28 through 31, we see the early church asking for boldness to preach because their lives were at stake. When you look at the Book of Acts, you read that their lives were being threatened. It wasn't a threat to get beat up or fired from a job. Their lives were literally on the line. Think of it in the context of threats on their lives if they preached the Gospel. They were asking for boldness to preach, so they wouldn't cower down or hide. If our lives were being threatened, we would pray that God would grant us, His servants, all boldness, so we will boldly proclaim the Word. The first disciples did. And the places where they preached were shaken, and they were filled with the Spirit of God. They lived in exciting times, seeing God move among them, but it was in a real life-threatening environment.

For us, it's more likely a matter of disobedience or possibly spiritual laziness. We are more likely dealing with obedience to His command and our willingness to preach than our lives being threatened. In most cases, our experience is a real contrast from those called to preach in the first century. How often do we ask for boldness? Are we bold after we learn an evangelistic program or after we've been filled with power? Prayer gives us vision and compassion to obey and go tell others. It gives us access to be filled with power to be bold witnesses and overcome all fear of preaching the Gospel to everyone. It's time for us to step out in faith—be obedient—and put ourselves in a place where we need to be asking for Biblical boldness. We can do it. We can step out and put ourselves in a place where we must rely on Jesus. We need to pray and put ourselves in a place where we need the Holy Spirit's boldness. We call it getting out of our comfort zone and trusting Him. God will work through us if we let him.

After the Lord Jesus had spoken to them, he was taken up into heaven, and he sat at the right hand of God. Then, the disciples went out and preached everywhere, and the Lord worked with them and confirmed his word by the signs that accompanied it.
Mark 16:19-20 (NIV)

God will confirm His Word as we go. If we desire to see God confirm His Word with power, we will need to be more intentional than ever, especially now that COVID protocols have separated people even more. The confirmation will not happen if we are not intentionally obedient to His Word. We must be intentional even more than ever. Many now use Zoom instead of going into the office. For our evangelism to be effective in our workplace with people telecommuting, we need to rethink our approach. Experts tell us there has been at least a fifty percent reduction in personal interaction in corporate America. How do we evangelize people that we can't physically be with?

I prayed specifically about reaching my coworkers during the shutdown of 2020. I prayed that God would increase my creativity. I made Zoom calls to specific individuals God placed on my heart when praying generally for my coworkers. As I prayed, creativity and wisdom from the Holy Spirit would come and reveal how to share and what to do. That would not have happened had I not been intentional with my prayers and time. As we approach the last days, we're moving forward in this fight of faith. There's no room to be less intentional. Evangelism must become our purpose in life—our vocation. Those who stumble often fall because they are unsure of their calling to preach the Gospel. They have not learned that their workplace is their mission field. Those who have discovered that their purpose is not to make a buck but to be ambassadors of the Good News of the Kingdom of heaven are becoming more intentional on the job. They are working with Spirit-filled boldness. They are on the front lines of the spiritual battle for the souls of men. They are confronting the enemy, casting out demons, laying hands on the sick, and God is making men and women whole.

You may have every desire to be used by God to transform lives today, but you may have questions like, "How do I overcome fear?" "How are we going to deal with rejection?" "What if I pray and nothing happens?" "How do I start a conversation about God?" I remember a time when I was so nervous; I couldn't speak. I've experienced rejection before; it wasn't fun. I never want to do that again. Who wants to go through that? One person I tried to share with cursed me out. It was a bad experience. I can't beat them up and make them listen to me, though I have thought about it. The experience made me hesitant to pull the trigger and approach the next person and share the Gospel again. You may have had similar experiences. Ask yourself the right question: "What if I pray and something does happen?"

The Art of Being Yourself

One of the biggest problems Christians struggle with is learning to be themselves with other people. Just be yourself and love people. It can be hard to be ourselves sometimes. At first, people often feel self-conscious and awkward when sharing the Gospel. As people learn to be themselves and to see the lost as wayward family members who need to be reconciled to God, the compassion of Jesus overcomes fear and hesitation. I didn't say the lost are our brothers and sisters in Christ. I am saying that we need to see them as who they can be potentially in Christ. It helps me relate to the lost around me if I see them as potential brothers and sisters in Him. They are wayward prodigals. Many are running from God, but it helps me speak to them as potential family in Christ.

If I look at them as if they were my own sister or my own brother, I can more easily be myself and love them with the love of God. It helps me to relax when I see the lost as someone soon to be in the family of God. I don't believe I am, or anyone is more or less valued by their economic state in life. It is only God's providence. I can easily be the one living in their situation.

We must see that person could be my father, mother, brother, sister, son, or daughter. Remember that when you see a drug addict or prostitute, see their brokenness and what the power of sin has done to them.

It is God's work; there is no pressure on me to have to make anything happen. I'm just having a conversation, and people respond. Don't complicate the conversation. Most often, simply being kind is enough to open the door or simply asking how their families and jobs are going. You can easily go from the natural to the spiritual. Most people can't see what they're missing. If they could see what they are missing, they would not be blind or dead in their sins. Ephesians Chapter 2 explains the problem. Why can't they see what is wrong? Because they are dead in their trespasses and sin. They're blind. If they could see, they wouldn't be blind anymore. We need to see through the eyes of God who they can become in Christ. This knowledge of man's condition with Jesus helps the compassion level stay high in our hearts. We need to be humble to know it because there's no difference between them and us, except now we can see. I once was blind, but now I can see because I am in Him. I can see now only because of God's gift of grace.

What happens when we relate to people by faith with grace? We make disciples. When you lead them to Christ, they put their faith and trust in Christ as Savior. It creates a natural transition to discipling them. Sharing with the intent to transform is not weird. Evangelism is not a sales technique. Leading someone to Jesus is not closing a sale. It is not a Jekyll-and-Hyde approach. You don't have to change personalities to preach the Gospel at work. Learn to be yourself. Enjoy God. Enjoy your life. Enjoy the opportunity to share God's love with a lost person—a coworker, a friend, a family member, or a neighbor. There is no pressure to make anything happen. Just be yourself. When someone receives Christ, it's just a continuation of your relating to them anyway. Witnessing can be a short-term or a longer-term relationship like you might have with a neighbor or coworker. If they're open, then great! If not, then share to the degree they are open to receive. But continually love them regardless of their openness.

Being yourself removes some of the weirdness that sometimes plagues Christians. Believers often have a hard time letting God use them. They don't know they can be used by God. Furthermore, they are trying to be something they're not. All God asks of us is to be ourselves. Be who God created you in Christ to be. Let your love shine through for others. Have the humility to remember there's just a thin layer of difference between them and us—the grace of God.

WHY NOT YOU?

When we approach people, we know three things people do not mind talking about. One is family. People don't mind talking about their families. I'm married. I have kids. I love to talk about my wife and kids. Are you married? Do you have a family? Do you have children? How many children? How old are they? We engage people on this level all the time. The second thing people, especially men, like to talk about is their jobs. What do you do professionally? Many men see themselves through the lens of what they do. It is easy to engage a man about his work.

The third is background. I grew up in the inner city. Others grew up on Long Island, in Chicago, or the Appalachian Mountains. Still, others grew up in the South. Everybody goes to church in the South—there's your way in. It is not a program, though. People can tell if you genuinely care. Part of being intentional is caring. We must be filled with His love to lead with His love. You started from the natural conversation, and now you can mention the spiritual because you found something in common. Your family went to church while you grew up, and so did the person you are sharing with. Move on by asking, "Do you still attend church?" or "When was the last time you attended church?"

The Gospel is the power of God. The Gospel is not sentiment that encourages churchgoing just to help improve your performance. We can't let them stay dead in their sins and not bring the Gospel that transforms. We're talking about bringing the Good News of Jesus Christ! Evangelism is preaching; witnessing is what we do. It is how we live. It's the lifestyle that can be extremely attractive to people that can open the door.

> *Go into all the world and preach the Good News to everyone. Anyone who believes and is baptized will be saved. But anyone who refuses to believe will be condemned. These miraculous signs will accompany those who believe: They will cast out demons in my name, and they will speak in new languages. They will be able to handle snakes with safety, and if they drink anything poisonous, it won't hurt them. They will be able to place their hands on the sick, and they will be healed.*
> Mark 16:15–18 (NLT)

Jesus told them to go into all the world and preach the Good News to everyone. Anyone who believes and is baptized would be saved, He told them, and anyone who refuses to believe would be condemned. He said miraculous signs would accompany—follow—those who believe. Jesus promised those who preach His Word would have His power. Anything poisonous won't hurt them. In addition to safety, He promised the power to make people whole. You will place your hands on the sick, and they can be healed physically, spiritually, and emotionally by the power of the gospel in Jesus' mighty name! Take the opportunity to ask people if you can pray for them. You will see God answer often and sometimes immediately.

This scripture connected to 1 Thessalonians 1:5 is crucial. Paul declared He came with power and with the Holy Spirit. This is what is lacking in so many approaches to preaching the Gospel. We need power and the Holy Spirit, not a program. Read this illustration, keeping in mind that we are talking about people versus programs.

This is not my story. A friend related it to me when he was with a Christian student on a beach during an evangelism training week. This is his story.

Bob and I met several religious skeptics and began talking about all sorts of things. Eventually, the conversation got around to Christianity, and it was a lively and invigorating discussion. We even exchanged addresses before leaving. I was feeling very good about the conversation, but Bob seemed very quiet. When I asked him what was wrong, he said, "I thought it was an absolute failure."

He went on to explain. "There are four major points to the Gospel, and you only brought in two of them. They weren't even in the right order." I said, "What were the names of the three people we met this afternoon?" "Oh, I don't know," he said. "What in the world difference does that make? I think there were two females and one male, or maybe it was the other way around." I stared at him in disbelief and sadness. He genuinely loved God; he was exceedingly religious and sincere. I doubt he ever missed his daily devotions, but he totally missed the entire point of our activity. He was sure of his agenda: his four points were his supreme value. His program was so rigid that real live human beings could not penetrate it. It may sound noble, but this is a kind of pharisaism, for it is so frequently the disease of the devoted.

This student was so busy rehearsing his four points of salvation that he forgot that he was speaking to the real people Christ had come to save. We must never forget that to be a follower of Jesus is to be dominated by love. We may not be well-versed in scripture or have a seminary background. We may be timid and unsure of ourselves, but we have arms and hearts meant to be used. We must ask ourselves, "Does my life reflect only religious activity? Or does it bear the mark of profound love?" When our lives are characterized by the love of Christ, we can begin to interest people in the Gospel. This young man's approach was a fantastic example of someone caught up more in the program than the person in front of him.

The terminology this guy was using, and his experience showed signs of pharisaism. He was attempting to convert the person to his way instead of leading him to Christ. We need to take heed. The Gospel is not about expounding what I learned in my evangelism training and getting through the main points. It is about really caring for the person in front of you. We need to ask ourselves, "Do I have real love? Am I being what Jesus would be to this person right now?"

1 John 4:17 says, "As Christ was in this world, so are we." That is one of the most powerful passages in the Bible, revealing how we live in this world today. As Christ was in this world, so are we. Do we see ourselves this way?

Programs vs. Prayer

As we continue to examine this concept of programs versus prayer, we will see that there are programs designed by men, and then there are God's programs. There's nothing wrong with our programs in themselves. It is not wrong to use a program. There are many different types of programs with differing degrees of effectiveness. Paul said in 1 Corinthians 2:4–5 that his message and preaching were very plain. Rather than using clever and persuasive speeches, he relied on the power of the Holy Spirit. The New Living Translation catches the nuance of his statements. He relied on the power of the Holy Spirit. He did this so we would not trust in human wisdom but in the power of God. Paul did this for his listeners' benefit. He came to them depending completely on the Holy Spirit and God's love for them. He relied on the power of the Holy Spirit, not on clever and persuasive speech.

Many programs and systems for sharing the Gospel have been developed over the years by men. Some examples that you might know of have been very popular. Evangelism Explosion (EE) was developed by Dr. D. James Kennedy. The Four Spiritual Laws was developed by Campus Crusade under the leadership of Dr. Bill Bright. The Roman Road; and Steps to Peace with God were developed by Billy Graham's ministry. The SALT conversation method starts by asking a question, then listening, and then talking (S A L T). This method provides an interview tool and a phone app that has been very effective on college campuses. The interview style works well with college kids. They are inquisitive and have a lot of questions to begin with. These are some popular evangelism methods. They have their place. I'm not antiprogram. I have used, read about, and studied all of these programs. The Spirit has given the founders of these programs some wisdom, I'm sure. They all began by praying, "Lord, what can I do to train others? What can I do to help people in evangelism?" God gave them the wisdom to put these programs together as a strategic approach. I'm not criticizing them, but they do not deal with the main obstacle to evangelism for most people. The main obstacle to sharing the Gospel is fear. Fear is the number one reason most people do not witness. Fear Factor may have been an entertaining TV show, but that fear factor also must be overcome to preach at work. Fear is a big hindrance to people sharing the Gospel because they fear being rejected. They are afraid to approach a stranger.

Fear is largely a delusion. Fear paralyzes because it makes what is hypothetical seem real. Programs help people overcome fear because it gives them something to lean on besides the hypothetical thoughts of what could go wrong. That's largely why people use them, and they can be effective.

There are too many Christians who have never led anyone to faith in Christ in their whole lives. Anything that encourages Christians to overcome fear, preach the Gospel, and spread the faith is a good thing. Many people want to share but are paralyzed by fear. They have never shared and don't know the pleasure of being used by God to change another person's life. Some reading this book fall into this category. You want to, but you never have. My prayer is that you take something from this book to inspire you to reach the souls around you. This is not condemning anyone because every believer wants to be used by God. There's no reason you can't experience the power of God flowing through you many times in your life. Many reading this book have led many people to the Lord. Everyone can begin today to be ambassadors of the Kingdom of Heaven.

If programs help people overcome their fear and organize their thoughts about the Gospel, then more power to them. When you are feeling nervous, or you find yourself in an uncomfortable situation, the scriptures you know, and the Gospel outline you have memorized can help you. Training to share the Gospel can be vital. That's what this book is all about. It's not on-the-job training, but it is encouraging you to be intentional and trust God. It's that simple. If we keep doing everything the same, everything remains constant. The results will be lacking. It's the same in our outreach and our personal desire to be used by the Lord. If I don't step out in faith and do something different, there will be nothing different to show for my efforts. Training can help people control their responses. You see it in the professional world.

WHY NOT YOU?

People work in different environments and professions that require controlled responses. The police, fire and rescue, and the military all offer specific training for the work they do. How do we deal with the human response? We train over and over and over. In a crisis, what do they fall back on? They automatically resort to their training.

We do this by teaching kids in our sports program. They practice fundamentals over and over and over. They say with sports, if you practice 100 percent in game speed, in real-life performance, you'll perform at eighty-five percent. The difference between practice and the real-time game experience is the nerves. The opponents aren't the same as your teammates that you normally train with. It's not a controlled environment. When the game is on, the need to rehearse becomes evident. Read testimonies about people's salvation. I have read every Gospel tract I could get my hands on for years. It helps me not ramble. Witnessing how God changed my life is a very significant part of sharing the Gospel. The more I practice, the better I get at relating the story of God in my life.

For example, in 2019 I contracted severe double lung pneumonia COVID. After I was hospitalized, I got worse and worse and began to die. While barely hanging on to life, I began feeling like I was leaving my body. I heard a voice say to me during that time that this sickness will not be unto death but for my glory. Three days later the Spirit of Gid came over my body and quickly healed me. My health and strength were immediately restored, and I was medically cleared to leave the hospital the next day! (by the way this is a true story). Sharing your story inspires others and reminds people how caring and personal God is and can be in their life also.

Sharing what God has done in you makes you Biblical and effective with other people. When they hear your story, of course, we often have to hear their story first. They can see what God has done in you. When you allow people to share their stories, you often get the privilege to share your experience. I've tried to get my story down to less than 200 words. I say, "I would not be here today if it was not for God. A while back, I started to leave my body, and I was dying. This is what happened to me …."

That's one way I can go. I have other stories I can use to gain people's attention and direct them to God. I should have been dead. I have had several near-death experiences in my life. In my marriage, this is what God did. In my family, this is what God did. We all have testimonies of the grace of God that we can share all day long. People need to hear what God has done in your life. You can intertwine the death, burial, and resurrection through your experiences, and you can demonstrate why Christ died for us.

I'm not opposed to programs, but we can't be putting our faith and trust in them. They can be a launching pad to get people going. Sometimes, I've taken a little bit of what I like from this program and some from that other one. I make what I share natural for me. One size does not fit all. God made you who you are, and He will use you as you feel comfortable being who He made you to be at work and as His ambassador where He has sent you. Some of you are shy. That's okay. You're probably a great listener. So many people today need a listening, caring ear. Then you will know exactly what to share with them about God's love for them.

Now, let's contrast all the programs of men with Christ's Holy Spirit. Christ's promised program is to be filled with the Holy Spirit and demonstrate His power as you go. Jesus shares the promised program in Luke 24. We see Jesus' promised program evidenced in D.L. Moody's life. Two Pentecostal sisters followed Moody around when he preached. They told him, "We're praying for you. He asked, "For what are you praying?" They said, "For you to be filled with the Holy Spirit." He said, "I already am filled with the power of the Holy Spirit." They said, "OK. We're praying for you." Over time, he fell under the conviction of the Spirit that he was not filled. This man received a baptism of the Holy Ghost and power..

It was very discernible in his ministry. He preached the same Gospel, the same sermons, but now severe conviction gripped the people he preached to. More people responded to the Gospel. It was the anointing of God in him. He thought he was filled with the Spirit, but when he totally yielded to God and allowed the Spirit to fill him more, his ministry changed. Now, he was baptized in the Holy Spirit, and with this new baptism, there was power with his message, and lives were transformed through his preaching.

We all preach the same Gospel message. You may come at it from any angle you want, out of your testimony or out of the situation in the person's life in front of you. You might be talking to him about marriage and show him scriptures about marriage. Next thing you know, the Spirit steps in and changes everything. You really can't do this without relying on God. We can show people the standard of the Word of God because that still brings them to understand. God has a lot to say, and He created us for these purposes. The Bible talks about every aspect of human life. You bring the Word of God into the conversation when you share the Gospel. D.L. Moody was filled with the Holy Spirit. It created a real zeal in him—a real fire in his ministry. The filling of the Spirit brought real fruitful results, and it will do that in you and me.

You may have experienced working in the Kingdom without power. We don't want to stay there. We want the zeal and commitment. The ministry of the Holy Spirit working in us and through us is indispensable. When we are filled with the Spirit, we expect the Father to be glorified in the Son. Is it our heart's desire to be used by God? Unless we implement change, nothing will change. Decisions form habits, and habits form character. Character affects our destiny and the legacy we leave. Character can impact eternity. It's not a light thing; making decisions to change affects eternity. Maybe not in your mind if you're born again, but certainly in others who are around us. It affects our loved ones—our family members. Luke 24:49 is a record of the last words of Christ before His ascension to heaven. It has been forty days since the resurrection. Second Corinthians 15 says there were 500 eyewitnesses at his ascension. He says: "Behold, I'm sending the promise of My Father." We know He gave the commission to go and preach repentance and forgiveness of sins. Here He is telling us that He is sending the promise. This is the difference between man's programs and Christ's promised program of the Holy Spirit. He will clothe you or fill you with His power to be a bold, fearless witness.

In Matthew 3, John said Jesus will baptize "with fire and the Holy Spirit." In Acts 2, that promise became reality. The Spirit came to grant Christ's followers power to be witnesses of Him. He baptized the first-century believers, and he baptizes you and me today. He wants us to be filled with that power. Two things are found in all four Gospels. One is that the death, burial, and resurrection of Jesus are mentioned in all four Gospels. Not all the parables and experiences of Jesus' earthly ministry are mentioned in all four Gospels. These three events are mentioned in all four Gospels because they are the essence of the Gospel message. The second thing found in all four Gospels is the baptism in the Holy Spirit. Being filled with the Spirit is just as vital as the death, burial, and resurrection of Jesus for our practical lives. He did everything He could do so we could be filled with His Spirit to complete the work of evangelism that He began on earth. The promised power of the Holy Spirit is mentioned in all four Gospels. (See Matthew 3:11, Mark 1:8, Luke 3:16, and John 1:33.) The Gospels connect the promise of the power of the Holy Spirit with the proclamation of the Gospel.

Jesus came to earth and ministered for less than four years. He departed, having completed the mission the Father sent Him to accomplish. He promised the Holy Spirit would come after His resurrection and ascension. The Spirit came in power on Pentecost. He empowered them then, and He empowers us today. Jesus completed His mission and has commissioned us to continue to share the Gospel with those in our times and our communities. Just as Jesus completed His mission by relying on the Holy Spirit, we must also follow His example to complete ours. The two things go hand in hand in proclaiming the Gospel.

The fastest-growing segment of the Body of Christ worldwide is those that would be called Spirit-filled. Not that it's a competition. Those who believe in the baptism of the Spirit are gaining the most ground in conversions when compared with other groups who do not insist on dependence and fullness of the Holy Spirit. My grandfather lived in Palestine. He was a Pentecostal pastor as well as an evangelist on the West Bank. It was a very tough area to evangelize. It was a tough mission field. He was part of the tiniest group of believers in Jesus Christ in Palestine. It was a humble life of near poverty. His passion for sharing the Gospel and living according to the Spirit compelled him. My dad was homeschooled, receiving no formal education other than what his dad taught him. My grandfather would go into the Muslim villages and preach the Gospel. They loved him. The Muslims respected him immensely. They called him Sheikh Boutros. "Boutros" was the Arabic word for Peter. "Sheikh" is a term implying respect and honor. It was not uncommon for my grandfather to pray eight hours a day. He would be called upon often to go to people's houses to pray. He cast out demons and dealt with other demonic manifestations. My grandfather was very bold. He'd go into Muslim villages where others were too scared to go because of the potential for persecution. My grandfather was filled with the Spirit and ministered in boldness that overcame fear.

We may have a theology, but our deeds and actions speak louder. If we allow fear to stop us, we will not see God at work. We have not received the Spirit of fear but of love (2 Timothy 1:7). Love conquers all—love for the Lord and love for the lost compelled my grandfather. Love should move us to be filled with the Spirit so we can see the power of the Gospel transform lives.

The ministry of the Spirit is also seen in John 14:16-22, where Jesus says He will ask His Father, and His Father will give us another just like Jesus. The word for "another" in Greek is "allos." The Spirit is another of the same kind, another helper Who will do in you and with you as Christ Himself would were He physically there with you. The Holy Spirit is given to those who obey Christ (Acts 5:32). It seems that not everyone obeyed His command, recorded in Luke, chapter 24, to go to the upper room and wait for the promise. Paul reports in 1 Corinthians 15:6 that there were 500 eyewitnesses of Christ. There were 380 who did not join the other 120 in the upper room, according to Acts 1:15. Maybe the John 14 passage is referring to the small number of those who did not leave but waited for Pentecost. The Holy Spirit was given first to those who obeyed Him. In addition, even after Christ gave the Great Commission (Matthew 28:18-20), not all went out and obeyed Him immediately (Acts 1:12-13).

One hundred twenty obeyed and went to the upper room and waited as commanded. Jesus instructed them to wait until they were endued, clothed with power from on high. It was not safe to profess Christ in Jerusalem after His death and resurrection. Jesus had commanded them to go into all the world, starting in Jerusalem, then Samaria, Judea, and the rest of the world. God may have given them an external influence called persecution to ultimately get them to go. After Pentecost, they went everywhere, and they went preaching. Soon, people were getting saved, and churches were springing up all over, like in Antioch. This is because of the ministry of the Holy Spirit, who was empowering them to go. They went not in their strength or with their strategy or programs. They went in the power of the Spirit.

The coming of the Holy Ghost came at a crucial time. The timing of the Holy Spirit in the wisdom of God is amazing because it was at Pentecost. It was during the Feast of Pentecost. According to Acts 2:11, the Jews, the proselytes, the Cretans, the Arabians, and others from different nations had come to Jerusalem for the feast. After they waited and the Spirit came, the 120 went out and began to engage all people from all over the world in their own language. They also performed signs and wonders as proof of the Spirit's power on them. The power of the Spirit that was promised to the first-century believers, and all called today by Jesus, enables them to intentionally go and fulfill the Great Commission to preach the Gospel to everyone, everywhere, every day. Why not you and me?

Being Ambassadors for Christ

Tom and Angela lived in their neighborhood for about twelve years without really reaching out to their community to get to know people. There lived in their own little world with no impact on their neighbors. Everyone in their community isolated themselves, content with playing in their backyards. Prompted by the Spirit, they decided to do something—to be intentional where they lived. They took all their gear they played with in the backyard and put all the play stuff in the front yard. They started engaging their neighbors like never before.

They became ambassadors of Christ to their community. They became intentional about meeting their neighbors and preaching the Gospel through their lives to them. In the parables of the Hidden Treasure and Pearl of Great Price (Matthew 13:44-45), you see two things happening. There was something found. One stumbled on a treasure in a field. The other was intentionally looking for what he found of value. Sometimes, even when we're not looking, we stumble on a soul who needs to hear the Good News. God sovereignly brings them our way, and we pray with them. We lead them to the Lord. We witness to or pray with them. That's the exception, not the rule! We're not called to hold back and just wait for that once-in-a-while situation. We're called to be like that merchant who was intentionally on the lookout.

The crowds with one accord paid attention to what was being said by Philip. When he heard him and saw the signs that he did, for unclean spirits crying out with a loud voice came out of many who had them.

Many who were paralyzed or lame were healed.
Acts 8:6-7

Notice two things that happened when Philip preached: demons were cast out, and the sick were healed. This is the testimony of Mark in his Gospel (Mark 16:20). This is what we are called to do. Go in power! If you start laying hands on people as you intentionally go out, God will confirm His words. We're not waiting on God to move like at Pentecost. The Spirit has come! His ministry is to baptize us with power so we can fulfill our mission. We no longer have to wait on Him. He's waiting on us.

Don't make yourself more accountable by reading this book if you are not going to step out in faith and obedience. Seriously, stop reading right here if you're not willing to be used by God. We all want to be ambassadors and go out in Jesus' name. We have nothing to offer people without the power of the Spirit but kind words and human sentiment. We need to give all our nothing to God because that's all we have to give. We thank the Father in Jesus' name for the opportunity to be used by Him. We pray the Lord would bless His people and be glorified as we obey Him through our words and our deeds. We asked the Father to show Himself mighty as we present ourselves to Him, as we look to His mercies, and present ourselves as offerings to be poured on the altar of faithful service to the Father. The goal in going with power is to reach lives and impact the world with God's love and the Gospel. We are called to advance the Kingdom and glorify His name with our obedience. We cannot hope to do this without being filled with the Holy Spirit and operating in His power. Going in power is the promised program of God to evangelize the world. Now, be filled with the Spirit and go in His power!

Lifestyle Evangelism

What are we talking about when we say the Spirit at work? This is the core concept of this book. We're talking about lifestyle evangelism. Being totally dependent on the Spirit is vital. Realizing that God desires to work through us is equally important. We must learn that being totally dependent on the Spirit. This means knowing that God wants to work through us, receiving how God's unconditional love transforms lives, and becoming aware of the perfect faith of Christ will help the supernatural become natural in our everyday lives. Lifestyle evangelism—being Spirit-led and Spirit-empowered—is the key to impacting our world for the Kingdom.

Being dependent on God is an essential part of the Christian experience. Our focus in this chapter is the fact that the Holy Spirit desires to work through us. What does He really want us to understand when thinking about evangelism and being dependent on God? Through complete reliance on the Holy Spirit, we will understand what the Spirit intends to do with us. The Spirit has already come; we are no longer waiting as commanded. He is waiting on us now! The reality is that God saved us for good works. God wants us to be zealous for certain things. Paul called Titus to produce Kingdom fruit that will remain. He declares much fruit will remain if we are active in our faith by believing God will lead us through the Holy Spirit to those He has appointed to be saved through us. Do you realize that there are lives that God has appointed to be reached through your life? These are the good works that Paul describes in Ephesians, Chapter 2. Good works have been prepared beforehand for us to walk in. We have been assigned to lead people to Jesus. We must be dependent on the Spirit to do this.

Ephesians 2:10 says, "We are His workmanship created in Christ Jesus for good works." This is not news to us. God prepared what we should do in advance—good works. We're saved for or unto good works. The beautiful thing about these good works is you don't have to hunt them down. We hunt God down, and He leads us. We move actively and intentionally by faith. As Mark 16 reports, this all relates to working with God. These good works are ordained, and those appointed will come to faith in Christ through you. They have been prepared ahead of time for us to walk in. We are His workmanship created in Christ. We have been transformed and renewed in Christ. We have been born again by the Spirit for good works. This is our purpose in Christ. We are called to be the men and women God has called us to be, doing the things He has set aside for us to do. It's a major part of the journey. He has set the course for our lives.

Good Works, Christianity, and Evangelism

I will take a detour to explain the proper order of good works. Most religions, even those based on the Bible, have some component of works to them. A common thread that runs through many religions is the process of doing good works to gain salvation. These creeds major on sacraments that must be performed in order to receive God's grace. Many people believe that at the end of time, they will be measured according to the good they have done in life. They hope that the good they have done will outweigh the bad. If they are good enough, they will get into heaven. This concept is illogical and not Biblical. No amount of good can cover or cancel even a single bad act. Most religions, except Biblical Christianity, include the focus on doing good works in order to be saved. Biblical Christianity admits that man can do no good because no man is good. All have sinned and fall short of God's glorious standard for good (Romans 3:23). No amount of good works will save someone. Good works are what the Christian does because God has made him good, like Jesus is good. He became sin for us so we could become righteous in Him (Ephesians 2:8-9). Christians do good works from the ground of being transformed by the grace of God by faith. Believers do not do good works in order to earn God's grace. Grace cannot be earned and is not deserved. Good works do not save. Believers do good works to bring glory to God and to fulfill their purpose as children of God. The difference lies between doing good works in order to be saved and doing good works because one is saved. God saves so that we can do the good works He has prepared for us to walk in. We do not do works to be saved.

What about the relationship between evangelism and good works? Have you ever asked yourself, "What is my purpose?" Walking in the good works He has prepared for us to accomplish is our purpose. Titus 3:8 reports, "This saying is trustworthy, and I want you to insist on these things so that those who have believed in Christ may be careful to devote themselves to good works." "To be careful to devote" means commitment. It shows intention.

WHY NOT YOU?

It is not an accident. These works, prepared by God for you and me, have been ordained for us to walk in. As we are devoted to Christ, we are to be devoted to His purpose for our lives. There are many excellent things that are profitable for us to do, but this is the purpose which defines us. The good works prepared beforehand for us to walk in can be done only by absolute reliance on the Spirit's direction. Only the Holy Spirit can lead us to the people God wills for us to reach. Only the Spirit knows the people God is already dealing with. He alone can lead us to be intentional in our prayers. We must trust Him completely to be intentional in our prayer life so He can use us. We must be led, directed, and guided by the Spirit as Jesus was. His direction can be instantaneous. You can engage a total stranger at the store who is assisting you in finding the perfect dress (or the perfect business suit, if you're a man). If you are intentional, it's not just about what you are getting from the person serving you. It's fulfilling your purpose to walk in the good works of evangelism every day.

I prayed with a man the other day at my house. He had never heard the Gospel before in his life. He came from Albania. He told me most of his nation has no clue about Christianity. I expounded the Gospel to him, prayed with him, and shared my testimony with him. I witnessed; I evangelized and gave him a Gospel tract. This man began to ask a lot of questions, demonstrating he was considering giving his life to Jesus. One sows, another waters. I watered this man. I also sowed seed into this man's life. I did everything to facilitate his coming to Jesus.

I shared the Gospel with him. I saw the wheels in his mind turning. The Good News was clicking with him. He wasn't ready to make a decision that day, and I was not forcing it. The decision doesn't save him. His faith and trust in what Christ did on the cross are where his salvation will come from. Don't ever make your witness about the decision. Closing the deal and getting a decision at any cost is always a temptation but leave the rest to God. Know that you helped them get one step closer to reconciliation with God. The acceptance, as in the act itself, has everything to do with the redeeming love of Christ. Be careful how you present the Gospel. Don't tell someone that repeating a prayer saves them. It doesn't. A prayer can be the medium to communicate with God. Prayer is just that, communication. It is not the act that saves! It is transferring their trust from self to Christ.

The Moravians are a great example for us. Count Zinzendorf was one of their leaders, and they experienced a one-hundred-year revival in Southern Germany. It was in the community of Herrnhut near modern-day Dresden.

About 600 people lived in this community. The amazing thing about the Moravians was that out of this community of only 600, they sent out 400 people as missionaries. Two-thirds of their population was sent out to evangelize. The home base of 200 supported the missionaries. They were extremely industrious. They experienced a 100-year prayer meeting revival. Some children were born into revival, and it was the only Christianity some of them ever knew. Some were born in a revival and didn't know anything else until they died and went to heaven! Why not us today?

Prayer and Evangelism

Prayer was their primary approach to the lost in their evangelism and discipleship. They would pray, "Father, lead me today to those that Your Spirit is already dealing with." I pray that God would lead me today to that person He is already dealing with. Lord, lead me to that person. That is being intentional and specific with prayer. That's being aware. Remember, if nothing changes, nothing will change. If your disposition is the same every day, nothing is going to change. If you go and come and aren't intentional in your prayers, don't expect people to be transformed through you. Once in a while, you'll run into someone ready to receive the Gospel. God, in His sovereignty, will not always wait on us. He is not above miraculously saving people with or without us.

I still hear some Christians testify that they have never led anyone to Christ in their lifetime. I ask, "When was the last time you prayed for a lost person? When was the last time you were intentional to witness?" Let me see your lifestyle—let me know of your prayer life—and I can tell how much you care for the lost. How much do you pray for the lost? Have you ever asked God to use you when you're going to run errands? He will show you connections. We're not here just to work, collect a paycheck, die, and return to dust. There are people appointed to be saved through your life. That's exciting news! There are those appointed whom you are supposed to lead to the Lord.

This is why we must pray to be used and be led to those that are lost. If this is on our minds, we are going to move in faith. If we're thinking about how we can let God use us to reach others, we're going to act in faith. Praying and going are acts of faith. We are lining our hearts up with God's heart. Faith is from God. All faith is from God. He's the author and perfecter of it, not us. If evangelism is on our minds, we're going to move in faith and rely on the Holy Spirit's guidance to connect us with those appointed to be saved through our lives.

When I'm coming and going, I'm thinking about those whom God wants me to reach. God has set people in my life for me to win. Who are they? We may not see everyone saved, but we're sowing the Gospel while we're on our journey. We're sharing and scattering seeds as much as we can. In doing this, we will discover those we are appointed to lead to Jesus. We don't just sit back in prayer, sitting on our hands in prayer. We are about the Lord's business, being intentional and expecting to connect with those the Father has ordained for us to reach. Not doing this is a painful thing to the heart of Jesus.

In 1 Corinthians 3:5-6, Paul's talking about jealousy. He is describing the rivalry that has sprung up among the followers of the Apostles. Some were saying, "I follow Paul." Others claimed they followed Apollos (verse 4). In verse 5, Paul declares, "Who is of Apollos? Who is of Paul?" They are servants through whom those people came to believe. As Paul confronts the competition among the Corinthians, he says that he and Apollos were only servants through whom they came to faith in Christ. Paul goes on to state, "As the Lord assigned to each." Some people are going to believe and receive Jesus. Some people have been assigned not only to Paul and not only to Apollos but to you and me to reach! They have been assigned by God in Jesus' name. They have been destined. We're called to reach them. It is vital that we see evangelism as a call on our lives. We need to see people come to faith in Christ. They believe through the influence of other people.

Ambassadors for God

We're ambassadors. Whether or not we are gifted to be evangelists, as in Ephesians 4, Paul calls us like Timothy to do the work of the evangelists (2 Timothy 4:5). We are called to be servants through whom others will come to believe as the Lord assigned to each. Paul says, "I planted, Apollos watered, but God gave the growth" (verse 6). Neither the one who plants nor the one who waters are anything—only God gives the growth. We are to be focused as servants or vessels through whom others believe. Who were the servants in your life that you believed through? You were their assignment. It's a divine assignment. God says, I've created you in Christ Jesus for good works, which were prepared, assigned beforehand—that you should connect with this neighbor of yours or a nephew. God's using us is so exciting!

Our purpose is to work together with God to reach people and fulfill our assignment. We set out to do it. We're intentional in doing the will of God. We walk in obedience. We're excited, expecting God to do some glorious things through us. We are all responsible to sow and to water so that we arrive at that assigned person.

How do we fulfill the purpose of God for us? We sow and water by sharing the Gospel. We do what we know to do. We walk in the revealed will of God. We go into all the world and preach the Gospel to everyone, every person. We spread the Gospel by scattering the seed of the Good News. As we scatter, those to whom we preach will be harvested into the Kingdom of God. They will come to believe and put their faith and trust in Jesus Christ as their personal Savior and Lord. We can't expect to see people saved if we sit on our hands in prayer. If we continue to live comfortable, cozy Christian lives, miraculous things are not going to happen. God can save with or without us, but most often, He uses people like you and me. Jesus, in sharing His parables about the Treasure in the Field and the Pearl of Great Price, describes men who discovered the Kingdom. These men were intentional. They bought the field or the pearl to gain the treasure that one stumbled over and the other finally found after a lengthy search. Don't wait to stumble over the people assigned to be won by you. Be intentional in your prayer life, praying and believing God will show you and God will use you.

God has created us for good works. He has prepared the good works that we are destined to do before we do them. God's love is unconditional, and Jesus' faith is always perfect. God wants to work in our lives through the Spirit to do His will. He has prepared good works beforehand for us to do. God desires us to be zealous. "[Jesus Christ] gave himself for us to redeem us from all lawlessness and to purify Himself a people for His own possession who were zealous for good works" (Titus 2:14). We are to be zealous for the works God prepared ahead of time. We are called and ordained to walk in these good works with passion. Some of the good works prepared ahead of time are people who have been assigned to us to reach with the Gospel. You may say, "Well, no one is assigned to me. I haven't met them yet." Is your life over? Are you still breathing? You are still here on earth to fulfill your purpose. If your purpose is done, then why doesn't God take you home? I had a near-death experience a little while ago. I know God spared me because there are people I am supposed to meet and introduce to the Lord. When my purpose is done, and I have completed my divinely appointed task, then God will take me home. I don't expect to go one minute before I finish the job God created me for.

So, I keep pursuing the will of God for me. As my pastor says, "If we get how God wants us, He'll get us where He wants us."

The Spirit Working Through Us

God wants us to know and learn how to rely on the Holy Spirit so we can understand that there are good works that have been prepared ahead of time for us to do. We're to be zealous for these good works. We're to lead those who have been assigned to us to the Lord.

The second aspect deals with the how. How can we see the Spirit working through us? How can we act so that a supernatural life becomes our normal life? The supernatural should be more real to us than what we see and understand with our physical senses. How do we start living in the supernatural? It most often includes two things. First, we must understand that God's love is unconditional. We must personally know, live, and understand there is nothing we can do to earn or lose our right standing with God except believe. Personally, experiencing the unconditional love of God is key to moving in supernatural faith. It is vital for faith to become a normal part of our lifestyle. Second, we must accept that Jesus' faith is always perfect. Yes, Jesus healed many because of their faith, but there were also many who did not have faith. They were demonized, blind, or simply at the end of their rope, but Jesus loved them and had enough faith for them to be made whole. He is the Healer, Deliver, and Savior of the world. How can we see the Spirit work through us? How can the supernatural become a normal part of our lifestyle? We must know God's love and believe that Jesus demonstrated perfect faith and will do the same through us as His available servants.

According to 1 John 2:27, God's love and anointing are already in us. You might say, "I don't feel anointed enough. I can't pray for anyone." Honestly, I didn't feel anointed the day I prayed with a lady, and that resulted in her salvation moment. I did not feel anointed at all, but I remembered it wasn't about me. It's never about us. It's about the person in front of us whom God loves. I'm conformable, knowing I can't save, heal, or fix anyone. I don't have to get worked up or feel any pressure. I don't have to get loud. I am free! I don't have to be proud. God resists the proud and gives grace to the humble. Humility is knowing that God loves the lost, and no one was lost or in need of salvation more than I was. God unconditionally loves them. God is seeking to glorify Himself in the situation. He simply calls us to move in obedience. The anointing is already in us. Jesus' love for the person is unconditional. Jesus always has enough faith to do miracles and bring salvation. He always has faith to answer our prayers. "Whatsoever things you pray according to My will, you shall receive them." Healings and words of knowledge (supernatural insight about the person's life) are common signs we can expect when sharing the Gospel. We are representing Jesus to all we come in contact with. God confirming His Word with signs and wonders is a natural result of faith combined with obedience. We often see healings following the proclamation of the Gospel. Words of knowledge are not uncommon when you are talking to strangers. God loves to demonstrate His love through us to others.

There is no faith without love. Without personally knowing Christ's love, there is no faith. Genuine faith flourishes when we discover God's unconditional love. Real faith ignites in us and flows through us when we understand God's unconditional love. It not only ignites us, but it shines through us to the person in front of us. "For God so loved the world." That's good because you and I wouldn't be here if not for that love. I'm thankful for that love. Genuine faith flourishes when we discover God's unconditional love for each of us personally.

Every hindrance is removed by knowing His love. Faith works by love (Galatians 5:6). What does faith work? Faith works the good works that were prepared before time, that were ordained by God for us to walk in (Ephesians 2:10). Among those good works are leading those assigned to us to come to faith. They are appointed to believe through your life, not just through Paul's or Apollos.' People are ordained to be saved through your influence.

Faith works by understanding and knowing that God is love, and His love has no conditions for salvation but repentance and believing. There are no conditions to God's agape love being expressed to anyone. "Freely ye have received, freely give" (Matthew 10:8). Many of us relate to God and each other with conditions. God needs nothing from us. There's nothing we can do to create value and worth in ourselves that would cause God to say, "Oh, you have that? Now I love you." We are dead in our trespasses and sins (Ephesians 2:1). No one seeks God. Every hindrance to faith is removed by God's love, for faith works by love. Agape puts value on the objects receiving the love without their having earned it. We need to stop trying to get what we already have in Christ. Stop trying to get what God already gave you and stop trying to be what Christ says you already are. Everything is finished in His eyes. It's a practical process in our lives. We are growing and becoming what He made us to be in Christ.

Understanding Who We Are

This is the identity crisis found in many Christians today. We need to understand who we are and the rights we have as children of God. Because of His unconditional love expressed at Calvary 2,000 years ago, we are His sons and daughters. This is the greatest expression of His love for us. We become His family. We become His loved ones. Trying to be what we already are in Christ leads to an identity crisis. We need to know God's desire to heal and deliver people because He loves them. If we really believe He loves, we will obey Him in confidence, representing God's love to others. God's love produces confidence. When you and I know we already have God's favor, we can go out as ambassadors expecting glorious outcomes that will turn hearts back to Jesus. This is what evangelism is all about—the lost getting found.

We already have favor in Christ. According to Ephesians 1:3, every spiritual blessing has been given to us in Christ. We don't have to pray to get a blessing; we need God to help us see more clearly what we already have in Christ so that we can share it with others. All blessings, power, and anointing have already been given to us. When you get intentional, guess what happens? We see more clearly what has been there the whole time.

I've run some struggling businesses in the past. The bank accounts were near zero. I remember when my dad turned over the barbershop to me. The account had some hefty coin in it. I thought that felt nice. Whatever I needed to get for the business, any upgrades I wanted, I could do. I just had to write a check. The money was there. It felt really good; it felt different. I was operating the business from a different position, a position of power, and not trying to hang on and micromanage every dime because the bank account wasn't full. We had to deal with what we had in hand at the time. This is the same thing. I didn't know it was there until I checked the bank account. I learned to ask God to help me see more clearly what I already am in Christ and what I already have in Christ to give to others. All power, blessing, and anointing have already been transferred to our account. Thank God for what we have already in Christ. Ask the Holy Spirit to open your eyes to see more clearly what you already have and who you already are.

"Blessed be the God and Father of our Lord Jesus Christ, who has blessed us in Christ with every spiritual blessing" (Ephesians 1:3). We have been blessed with every "spiritual blessing." It does not say "natural blessings." We're talking about spiritual blessings here. You can sell out for the temporal and carnal if you want, but that's inferior, extremely inferior. Fleshly blessings will do nothing for your soul. They may stroke your ego but not fill your soul.

> *For Jesus Christ, the Son of God does not waver between yes and no. He is the one whom Silas, Timothy, and I preach to you. As God's ultimate yes, He always does what He says. For all of God's promises have been fulfilled in Christ with a resounding yes, and through Christ, our amen, which means yes, ascends to God for His glory.*
> 1 Corinthians 1:19-20 (NLT)

All the promises of God have been fulfilled in Christ. All the promises of God are already ours. Let me write it again: All the promises of God are already ours. We don't have to wrestle them out of our dad's hands. It is God's nature to bless, and He desires to share with His children. We're not fighting Him. We're not trying to get ourselves in a certain position or create some kind of intrinsic value or worth within ourselves. We can do nothing that would make God say, "Because you have worked so hard, now you can have My unconditional love." That's not how it works. We need to get our minds renewed. All the promises of God are already ours. They're not earned. They don't need to be earned. They are all shared with us through grace. All of the benefits as children of God belong to us in Jesus. Once we understand that all the promises of God are ours, we will want to live obedient lives. When you understand God's love, you're not going to become less obedient. You're going to want to be more obedient to Christ and represent His finished work on the cross more effectively. We obey because the promises are already ours. They are already yes and amen in God's eyes.

Is it my faith or their faith that saves? Is it our faith or their faith that will get them healed? It doesn't matter; it's Jesus' faith. Jesus Himself is the source of all faith. Faith is not an effort on our part to have confidence or act boldly. Faith totally relies on God's love that has already been proven on the cross. Faith trusts in what God's grace has already provided (Ephesians 2:8-9). When we realize this, the struggle ends. Hebrews 12:2 reports that Jesus is "the author and the finisher of our faith." We rely on Christ's perfect faith. You might not have the faith you need to raise a dead person or heal a crippled leg. I never thought I did. There have been times when I have felt faith rise up in me, and there have been times when I've had no feeling of faith rise up in me. As my pastor has said, "When you don't have adequate faith, rely on obedience." Just do what you know to do. Do the Word. Obedience is moving in faith. All of God's promises are yea and amen. Whether you have faith or not doesn't matter. Jesus does, and His faith is perfect. All the unsaved people we're praying for don't have faith, not yet. Don't look at their faith; they don't have any. The miracles don't come when you're full of faith but when you obey the Word. That's powerful. Rely on God's unconditional love and perfect faith in Christ for them.

Ephesians 3:20 says, "[He] is able to do exceedingly abundantly above all that we ask or think, according to the power that worketh in us." I prayed like this for a lady I was sharing with: "Lord, I know You love this lady. You died for her. Her back is hurting her; she's been seeing doctors with no help. Please confirm Your Word and heal her." I hadn't preached the Gospel to her yet. There were no steps she had to go through. God moved, and out of her own mouth, she confessed that Jesus healed her. She was ripe to hear the Gospel now that she experienced the power of God in such a tangible way!

Mark mentions two things in his Gospel (Mark 16:15, 20). First, he says, obedience is man's part. Second, the miracles are God's part. It says in verse 20 that God was working with them. Verse 15 commands us to go into all the world and preach the Gospel. In verse 20, they obeyed. They went everywhere. Obedience was their part. What happened when they obeyed? God moved! They proclaimed; they preached the Gospel. What did God do when they proclaimed the Gospel? He worked with them to confirm His Word. What will God do when we proclaim the Gospel? He works with us to confirm His Word.

A friend of mine was sharing a testimony of setting his mind to simply obey God and preach the Gospel. What did God do? God worked in and through him. He shared the Gospel with a visiting relative. Because he set his heart on God's purpose for the person in front of him, God moved. It doesn't have to be difficult. Let it be a natural part of your lifestyle. When you go to the grocery store, there's a counter there. Engage the clerk with kindness. Say, "Hi. How are you? How's your day today?" The clerk is just standing there all day. No one is talking to him for the most part. You are going to stand out because of your kindness. He may say, "Yeah, my back is really hurting. I've been standing on my feet all day." You say, "Sir, can I pray for you?" Lay your hands on him. Pray for healing and be equipped for some follow-up. Maybe you are seed-sowing. Be prepared when you go to proclaim the Gospel for glorious things to happen. Miracles will follow faith and obedience. God will work with you. God will work with each person who purposes to proclaim the Gospel. God will do the same as you read in Mark's Gospel. Jesus is the same today, yesterday, and forever (Hebrews 13:8). We're not waiting on God: He is waiting on us to go so He can work with us.

We're not waiting on God: He is waiting on us to go so He can work with us. This is what Mark 16 is sharing. The disciples went out and preached everywhere. God's love has no interest in what anyone can do. It has no conditions and is solely based on who He is. God is love. First, John 2:27 reveals the anointing you receive from God abides in you. And 1 John 4:17 reports that His perfect love is expressed perfectly through us. Being equipped to preach the Gospel is a process. A large part of the process is us responding to God in obedience by faith. First, John 4:17 is one of the most powerful scriptures in the Bible. It says: "As He is, so also are we in the world." Are we vessels of the Holy Spirit or not? Are we one with the Father? Are we children of God? Is He in us or not? Are we heirs and joint heirs or not? We're representatives of that unconditional love everywhere we go. Christ is in us.

Go in Power

In John 10:25, Jesus is having an encounter with the Pharisees. He said, "I spoke my words to you, and you do not believe. Jesus did more than preach; He went from words to signs and wonders. Jesus declared, "The works that I do in my Father's name they bear witness about me." Part of the witness is the signs that follow. These signs shall follow those who are obedient to Him. "If I am not doing the works of my Father, then do not believe in Me" (John 5:38). Jesus is saying if you're not going to believe the words, then you're nitwits. You're blind. You can't deny the miracles I perform right in front of your face. These miracles are real! Even a nitwit who is spiritually blind and arrogant can see it. Jesus said you can't deny them. He reported that even if you don't believe Him because of His words, you ought to believe because of the power of the works that He does.

A Muslim lady believed the works, and without our even telling her, she said Jesus healed her. Muslims believe in Isa; they call Jesus "Isa," meaning "great prophet," but they don't see Him as God in the flesh. Jesus told the Pharisees, "Believe the works and understand that the Father is in Me, and I am in the Father." Jesus was calling them to rely completely on the Holy Spirit. It gets fun when you trust the Spirit. You can't be lazy. There are times when you don't feel like obeying. Remember, it's not about how you feel. When you make it about God's unconditional love and Jesus' perfect faith, you change so God can change the one you are preaching to. Jesus is the author and the finisher of our faith. Some translations say "author and perfecter" of our faith. He begins the process, and He completes it. Don't make it about you or your faith. Make it about God's love, faith, and power working through us. God loves everyone. We're just ambassadors of His love.

Going in His power is the game changer in our evangelism. We cannot do it, so stop trying. Stop waiting on God and step out in faith, relying solely on the Holy Spirit, and He will demonstrate the Father's love and His power to transform lives. If we do not depend on the power of the Holy Spirit to go with us and do the works prepared for us, we are entering battle unarmed, and we will lose. Go with the love, faith, and power with which God has equipped you. Discover your destiny in doing the good works God has made for you to do. Experience a Spirit-led life that reaches everyone, everywhere, every day.

Reaching Our Neighbors & Coworkers

Reaching our neighbors and coworkers is where the rubber meets the road in our lifestyle evangelism. Because these are the people with whom we spend over a third of our lives, it is vital that we reach them. God has strategically placed us where we live and where we work. It is His providence that you got that job where you work. You may think you earned it, or your credentials made the way for you. That may be part of it, but the bottom line is God put you there! You may think you have found the house of your dreams or that you are stuck in the neighborhood where you live. Divine insight tells us that you live where you do because it is God's plan. It may not be your plan, but it is God's sovereign plan. God has placed you where you live and where you work to reach those you work with and those you live nearby. He has divinely put you where you can do the most good for His Kingdom. It is vital that we see reaching our neighbors and our coworkers with the Gospel as the good works that God has created for us to walk in. Where we work and live gives us access to reach lives with the Gospel.

Even today, with so many working remotely from their homes, about one-third of our lives is spent in the workplace. If you don't work outside the home, your neighbors are like your coworkers. There are still plenty of opportunities if you do not work outside the home. There's no limit to the opportunities that present themselves for us to reach our coworkers and our neighbors. The limit is only in the degree we're willing to be creative and get out of our comfort zone. It's as simple as moving your family activities from the backyard to the front yard. I know some people who put the kids' toys in the front yard instead of the back, and as they played in the front instead of the backyard, the neighborhood kids started hanging out with their children in the front yard. Adult neighbors began stopping by. The evenings in their front yard turned into a block party for outreach and celebration. They got to know their neighbors by establishing relationships in casual play and conversation. The simple act of moving from the backyard to the front opened the door for sharing the Gospel. It is an easy next step to launch a monthly gathering—a Bible study for outreach. There are a lot of things we can do if we're willing to put ourselves out there. We will see God do amazing things through our lives if we are willing for Him to use us! People are always stopping by where we live to tell us something. I've had so many opportunities to pray with them. Simply offer them a drink to take along and ask them how their job is going. Some believe to saving faith, and others receive a Gospel tract.

There are three aspects to consider when we reach out to our neighbors and coworkers. The first one is Paul's example, Serve to Win. The second is Mind the Gap. The third is Practice Hospitality.

Serve to Win

1 Corinthians 9:19–23 (ESV) reveals the secret to the first step in reaching our coworkers and neighbors: "Serve them to win them." It's what the apostle Paul referred to six times in this passage. "For though I am free from all, I have made myself a servant to all, that I might win more of them. To the Jews, I became as a Jew in order to win Jews. To those under the law, I became as one under the law (though not being myself under the law) that I might win those under the law. To those outside the law, I became as one outside the law (not being outside the law of God but under the law of Christ) that I might win those outside the law. To the weak, I became weak, that I might win the weak. I have become all things to all people, that, by all means, I might save some. I do it all for the sake of the Gospel, that I may share with them in its blessings" (ESV, emphasis mine). Paul declares six times in these verses his desire to win souls. He is setting the example to acquire souls for the Kingdom. The word translated "win" in 1 Corinthians 9 is the same word translated as "gain" in the synoptic Gospels when Christ asked, "What shall it profit a man if he shall gain the whole world, and lose our soul?"

I believe Paul's motive in using the same word that Jesus did was to contrast the gain of souls with the gain of the world and the things of the world. What is the true eternal treasure? What are we living for? The depth of our value system is revealed by the time and commitment of what we do on a regular basis (Luke 12:34). Paul is deliberate in his phrasing. He is establishing the motive behind his actions. He answers the why. Paul gives us the answer to why he's doing what he's doing. What motivates him? What's his driving force? Why be a servant to all? He unequivocally states, "That I might win more. That I might win them."

WHY NOT YOU?

Why did Paul become a Jew to the Jews? In order to win Jews to the Messiah. Why did he act as if he was still under the law? That he might win those under the law. To those outside the law, he becomes as one outside the law that he might win them. Again, why did he become weak to the weak? That he might win them, too. Paul wraps it up in verse 23: "I do this all for the sake of the gospel." His goal is winning them. Winning them is going to happen when he serves them. He serves them to win them, is what he says. "I have made myself a servant to all in order to win more of them." Why? Everything he does is for the sake of the Gospel. Paul is confessing that he takes on the role of Christ, becoming a servant, because serving helps him win more people. This is his evangelistic strategy. Serve to win!

When was the last time you served somebody to win them? I'm not talking about in church to our fellow Christians, although that is needed and should be done. When was the last time you served a sinner? When was the last time you served, knowing you were not getting anything back like the Good Samaritan did? You may not even receive the satisfaction of seeing them edified. When was the last time? Are you willing? Would you drop everything to serve another? The true follower of Christ does it all the time. That's who Christians are and what they do. The apostle Paul is asking, "When was the last time you served someone that you normally wouldn't?" It doesn't have to be only the destitute, poor, naked, and blind. We don't have to go to Africa. Darkness covers the whole world. People are broken, lonely, and hopeless everywhere. The opportunity to serve is right in your neighborhood and your workplace.

Paul is very insightful about what kind of man God has made him. He is provoking us to serve them in order to win them. He says he serves all. What does that look like as it pertains to our coworkers and our neighbors? What does it look like? How does that translate to you and me? You and I need to be asking Jesus that question and pray for wisdom and direction. If you've determined not to get out of the boat, don't pray because you're wasting your time. If you're open to being used, then pray. God will speak to you, and you will see great things happen if you obey.

Availability is the most important aspect of evangelism. Just simply being available is the best thing you can do. You have experienced the Gospel. You know the Gospel. You have a heart to share the Gospel and be used by the Lord. Being available is key, being available throughout the day, being available in the highways, at Sam's Club, and then back to Marshall's. Paul does a fantastic job giving us insight into why he does what he does. I would encourage you to look at these passages. We are not better than Paul or Jesus, who came to serve others (Mark 10:41-45). Paul was the apostle to the Gentiles, unbelievers. He went to the nasty sinners in Corinth, where more than 1,000 temple prostitutes, both male, and female, serviced patrons of the idols. It was known and had a reputation in the Roman world for being a crude, vulgar city. Paul planted a church there. What about you? Where are you serving? What are you doing right where you live, in your neighborhood where everybody looks happy and comfortable? All it takes is a little tweak in your disposition and a real willingness to get vulnerable to reach out to your neighbors. Some of you are doing that. Build a little relationship and learn how to mind the gap.

Mind the Gap

Mind the Gap is the next step in strategic evangelism. In the London subway, you are told to "mind the gap" at every step. There are signs everywhere that read, "Mind the gap." What happens if you don't mind the gap? You might get hurt! To mind the gap means to watch your step. It is important to watch where you put your feet. There's a gap between the train and the sidewalk when you get on and off the subway. We call the high speed train "the metro" where I live. There's a gap where you can get your foot stuck or stumble. We should be "Minding the gap" in our evangelism.

We mind the gap by first having our mind set on the space of the sinners who are separated from God eternally. People around us are separated by their sin from God. There's a great gap and distance between them and God. Christ has come and provided reconciliation. He has made peace with God for man. Reconciliation is available to everyone. We need to preach this Gospel to ourselves. We need to be refreshed in the joy of our own salvation. When this is set in our minds, we're going to be thinking about this great gap of separation from those around us. As I meditate on what God has done through Jesus Christ, the coworkers I see on a regular basis or talk to on the phone come to mind. I consider the gap between them and God and their eternal separation from God (Luke 16:26). We are in contact with people every day who are separated from God. Many Christians tell me, "I have no problem starting a conversation, but to transition the conversation from the natural to the spiritual is where I get scared." Most people today are spiritual in some way or another. Simply bring God into the conversation. Some people find it difficult only because they're expecting a bad outcome. They let fear invade them, and they are paralyzed to go further with the Gospel.

Let's look at how Ezekiel 22:30 reads in the New Living Translation: "I looked for someone who might rebuild the wall of righteousness that guards the land." Lord, help us to embrace Your heart. This is God's word to the prophet. God is saying, "I looked for someone who would rebuild the wall of righteousness." Righteousness comes only from Jesus. We're righteous because of His righteousness. It doesn't happen any other way. Righteousness "guards the land." The prophet says God searched for someone. He looked for someone. It was a concentrated effort by God. He looked for someone "to stand in the gap in the wall" so He wouldn't have to destroy the land, but He found none. God is not willing that any should perish. He said, "I take no pleasure in the death of the wicked." He doesn't want to bring judgment. It is part of God's character. He is just. Exodus 34 tells us He's merciful; He's compassionate. God is longsuffering; He's faithful by no means clearing the guilty. He's just. He must punish sin, and He did. It was put on Jesus for you and me. He searched for a man or a woman. He looked, but He found none. There was no one to stand in the gap.

Break it down to your daily life. Take it one day at a time. We wake up today and live our lives. Do we consider the eternal gap, the eternal separation of God and our coworkers, family, neighborhood, and friends? Did we think of God wanting to reach them? Did we think about it one time today? Did we even take it into consideration? We went about my normal schedule. We breathed the regular life that God gave us. Every breath is a gift of grace. What are we doing with that gift? Are we comfortable building our Kingdom while God is asking, "Who is going to build Mine?"

I was meditating yesterday, and it hit me that God is a spirit. He doesn't live in a body. We're His body. He manifests Himself and accomplishes His purposes and will through the body of believers, His church. He needs a body. He works with the body. His Spirit lives in the body. Who are we? Are we the Body of Christ? When you think of the Body, don't think only of the church as an organization and the things that a church does. The church is a living, life-flowing organization. Think of Whom we're representing and what God wants to do by the Spirit through us. Think from God's perspective. Once we are saved, it is church, church, church. Jesus didn't bear the shame and pain of the cross for us to sit comfortably in a building. You were baptized into the body, and He places you in the body to be discipled and to edify each other. But we can't gain a whole bunch of knowledge and just sit on it. God found none. We need daily to "mind the gap." Let it ever be in the forefront of our minds and our hearts. How does that work? How do we "mind the gap" every day? We simply need to pray, asking God for wisdom. "Lord, how can I reach my neighbors?" "Whatsoever things you ask according to His will, He hears us (1 John 5:14- 5). He will answer. Start praying this way if you are not already. When you do, expect God to move. When we pray according to His will, the first thing that happens is we are changed. The Psalmist said, "Before I teach sinners and transgressors the way, convert me" (Psalm 139). When I am converted, the Lord changes my mindset and my disposition. When we pray, "Search me, Lord. See if there is anything in me that would prevent you from using me. Lord, change me," He changes my attitude. Help me to mind the gap. Help me to set before me, daily, my neighbors, their condition, and their eternal souls. You have put me in this neighborhood, not because of the four bedrooms and three baths. I came for the comfort; You brought me to win them to You. I came for the picket fence. You brought me to reach these souls."

I don't write this to condemn. I communicate the heart of God to remind you who you are in Christ. God wants to express Himself through your life visibly. The only question that remains is, "Are you available?" Are you willing to be and do what He made you to be and do? The moment you make yourself available, He's going to share His heart with you. God is going to give you the basic instructions on how to reach your neighbors and coworkers.

In my many trips to Africa, there were two years in which I led teams for mainly evangelistic activity. After every crusade, in every town we went to, hundreds of children would show up. I said, "We're not turning the kids away; we have to minister to them. I looked to the team members who were gifted to minister to kids, those for whom serving children was their world. We preached and invited people to receive Christ. We prayed with them. We were wrapping things up one night, and I said, "You two, why don't you minister to those kids?" There were 300 kids in that village. It was a suburb packed with people. The children's team took off! They preached the Gospel. They shared Jesus in a childlike way with children. They had a blast!

When I got on the plane after that trip, I asked the Lord, "Do we really have to go all the way to Africa to see Your Spirit move? Are You not the same around the world? Are You not omnipresent? Are you not the same everywhere? Are we so blinded by our prosperity, Lord, that we can't even see the need around us?" I prayed right then and there, "Lord, if you show me what to do, I'll do it. I don't care what it is. I want to see You move at home like You moved in Africa. You're the same everywhere. Move in my neighborhood." I told the Lord in that prayer that I know there are a ton more people in Africa that need Him, but what about my neighborhood? It is where I live; You put me there. I don't know what to do. Everyone's locked in their homes, in their comfort zones, sitting on their six-figure incomes. I don't know what to do to reach them. I prayed, "If you show me, Lord, I will do it." I was weeping as I prayed. I'm on the plane, and I'm crying. Then I heard one phrase: "The kids."

I heard the Lord give me the secret to reaching my neighborhood. It was, to begin with, serving the children. There were tons of kids in my neighborhood. He told me to start with them. It was late in the year, and what better time to serve my neighbors than the holidays? Since that time, we've learned how to reach them as a community more effectively. There was a time at Halloween when we'd shut the door and turn the lights off. I proclaimed, "I'm not participating in that demon-inspired Day of the Dead!" Halloween is the one holiday celebrated in America when people come knocking on your doors. They don't know it, but they're trying to get evangelized, and we're shutting the door in their face because the holiday is wicked! We can become so separated from our neighbors. On Halloween, we lock the door and turn off the lights. "Shh! They might think we're home!" They know you're home! Every kid can tell who's home and who's not. We did leave some candy on the porch. The whole container was gone with the first group.

I saw a house in a friend's neighborhood that had neon lights all over the trees and all over the house. I said, "If this dude can light up Halloween for all this gory darkness, goofy stuff, then why can't we lift up Jesus, who is the light of the world?" He gave me one of the craziest ideas I ever had. I learned a lot from that guy. I stopped, and I watched his exhibit. I saw what he did. He used fluorescent paint on everything and shined fluorescent lights. So, I went to Home Depot. I bought wood to build a cross big enough for Arthur Blessitt to drag around. I spray-painted it florescent pink. I bought blue lights and put them on the posts. It was a big cross. I got big nails and put them up on the cross. I draped a cloth on the back, put it up with rope, and pulled it up. My girls helped me. I was telling them the resurrection story while we were building the cross. I put the lights on and borrowed the angel outfits used for the play at church. My girls wore them. I put the cross at the end of the driveway and put a basket at the bottom of the cross with a little note.

Everyone who wanted candy had to kneel before the cross. That's where they should be bowing. When they were getting the candy, they saw the little sign, "Jesus died for you. He loves you." All the kids would read it as they came to get candy on Halloween. Guess who was floating around the cross. My girls were, dressed like little white angels. When the lights shined on them, they were illuminated like the cross. They look like bright angels on fire with all the extra lights. People didn't know what to do with it. I met people at the driveway, and some were scared until they got closer. Then they understood. It could have been interpreted as one of the goriest and cruel things—a cross on Halloween. I told them, "Yeah, a cross on Halloween!" The people started getting it. Some people were freaked out. They were like, "Are you serious?" The kids loved it. It opened doors for us to share the Gospel at Halloween. We were minding the gap and serving all so we could win some.

One time at Easter, we opened the garage door, put a backdrop up, and brought the TV out of the house. We set up seats outside in the front for the kids to watch. We played and sang some Easter music, and all the little kids were singing with us. We cooked hot dogs and showed a movie about the resurrection. The first year we had fifty people at the house. The next year it was 100 people. We showed a video about Christ's redemption and talked about the true meaning of Easter. We had some friends help and pray with us. In the third year, we took it to the church to have more room, and it became the church's annual Easter Resurrection Celebration outreach. The first year, one of my neighbors (an ex-cheerleader for the Redskins) was born again at our house. She later led her husband to the Lord. They led both of their kids to the Lord and are raising them in the Word. Their daughter is a missionary on the mission field now. One little measly outreach with our two dimes or two little pennies that we offer up to God because that's ultimately all we have to give. It's all nothing, but when you step out in faith with nothing, God does a whole bunch of miracles with it. All we have to do is move according to what God tells us. Lives will be touched with the Gospel because of the power of God.

Practicing Hospitality

We have discussed serving them to win them, and we have looked at minding the gap that separates the lost from the Father. The third aspect of evangelism I want you to consider is practicing hospitality.

WHY NOT YOU?

I come from a Middle Eastern culture, and the Arab culture is known for its hospitality. It's a deep part of everyday life there, and my family practiced in all my life. If you didn't eat half a leg of lamb when you came to our house, my mom would think something was wrong. My family knows how to practice hospitality properly, and my mother was an incredible hostess who loved serving others. I grew up with this Middle Eastern mindset of hospitality. When I researched some of the outreach strategies of the early church, hospitality was one of their primary methods of winning people to Christ. We serve them so that we might win them. It doesn't always mean raking your neighbor's yard or helping them paint the house. It certainly could involve those things, and those things have been very effective, especially for youth groups. But just being available and minding the gap is where it begins. It can be as simple as starting a conversation and showing them some kind of care. People will talk readily about their jobs, their family, and their backgrounds. Remember these three areas people love to talk about.

A key time to look for is when your neighbors are in crisis. A crisis of life is when people are in the most need and welcome help from even strangers. Issues out of our control come up in people's lives. If you have some relationship already, it makes it easier to share God's love with them. I have brought pizzas to neighbors, prayed with some, and even performed funeral services for some who've lost loved ones. All this is the result of reaching out, being kind, and showing interest in their lives, knowing God put me there to serve them. People are open to the Gospel during times like this. Simple hospitality is where you can really make headway for the Gospel with your neighbors.

The holidays are also great times to serve. People are already feeling very festive. Special occasions are great opportunities to show hospitality that leads people to Jesus. Christmas and Easter are already Christ-centered times. I was certainly impacted during those times in my own life. Those are times when people think about the Lord. Many of them are even open to going to church during those seasons. Hospitality was one of the primary methods of evangelism in the early church. They used the associations with people they were already attached to. There were social gatherings with purely social emphasis, but they also evangelized through those social associations. They had already established relationships at work. These became natural connections for sharing the Gospel. They would serve people and see them come to the Lord. It is the same as practicing hospitality in your neighborhood.

Indonesia is not an Arab nation, but it is the largest Muslim-populated country in the world. How did Indonesia become the largest Muslim country in the world? It wasn't one of the nations that Mohammad went to and spread Islam back in the sixth and seventh centuries. How did Islam spread so well in a non-Arab country? How did Indonesia become the largest Muslim nation in the world? Well, when the people of Indonesia were asked if the Christians had come, they said, "Yes. They built their churches and invited us to come. But the Muslims worked with us and lived with us." It was strategic. Belief made no difference. Christians, especially in America, have created a secular/sacred dichotomy separating their spiritual life from their work lives. Muslims see the secular as sacred, and they penetrate every area of society to spread their religion. It is a false religion, but they are passionate about it. Much can be done with passion. We can learn from the zeal of Muslims to invade our culture and become all things to win some.

Christians have had a lot of success worldwide setting up hospitals. Few atheists have done good in this world like Christians have. The majority of people laying their lives down, doing good in the world, are Christians. Believers in Jesus are laying down their lives so others can live every day. Hospitality is powerful. When was the last time you invited a neighbor over for a barbecue or a coffee in your home? Many of your neighbors do not know another believer in Jesus. Take the opportunity to invite them into your home. Move the toys from the backyard to the front yard. Meet and greet your neighbors. Get to know them and then do a little something for them. Serve them. Invite them to be part of your life and to church. Mind the gap of their separation from God. Let the knowledge of their potential for perishing invade your everyday thoughts. Think of them; serve them. Show hospitality to them. Love them as you would, family. Begin with something small, like a backyard cookout. Let it build off that. Then you can invite them to church or start a short Bible study. "Hey, we're going to hold a meeting once a month at 7:00 for a thirty-minute gathering." Keep it simple. Ask, pray, mind the gap, and say, "What can I do, Lord? I'm available. What is it, Lord, you have for me to do?" Build off the little things.

"Hospitality" is an interesting word. It means the "friendly and generous reception in the entertainment of guests." Hospitality can be inconvenient. It is not convenient to show you care and serve your neighbors, but hospitality is an effective part of evangelism. Paul said, "I serve them that I might win them." He became all things to all men for the sake of the Gospel. Hospitality is the "entertainment of guests, visitors, or strangers.

WHY NOT YOU?

Entertaining strangers is an interesting concept. One of the key definitions of the word in the Greek word for hospitality is "to entertain strangers." Hospitality means entertaining strangers.

> *When God's people are in need, be ready to help them.*
> *Always be eager to practice hospitality.*
> Romans 12:13

The call of the Christian is to serve with hospitality. The writer reinforces the obligation in Hebrews 13:2: "Don't forget to show hospitality to strangers." We are to serve and associate with everyone, not only Christians, for the sake of the Gospel. When we entertain strangers, we discover that "some who have done this have entertained angels." We cannot forget to show hospitality.

> *For I was hungry, and you gave me food, I was thirsty, and you gave*
> *me a drink, I was a stranger, and you welcomed me.*
> Matthew 25:35

What if a family from Afghanistan moved into your neighborhood? They don't know anybody. They're out of place. Here's an opportunity to welcome people who might already be uncomfortable being in a new community. Here is a chance to win them. Jesus said, "I was a stranger, and you welcomed me." Are you welcoming? Are you practicing hospitality? There are so many ways to do it. Use your imagination. Ask God to show you and open the doors to serve your neighbors and coworkers. Mind the gap! We get to practice hospitality and serve them in order to win them to Christ. It's easy to share God's love with others.

Before we can transform our neighborhood and coworkers, we need to be transformed ourselves. The Psalmist says, "When I'm converted, I will reach sinners in the way." As you ask, you will receive, and you will see lives touched. Wouldn't it be fantastic to lead one of your neighbors to Christ? You can, and you will. There's no reason that you shouldn't expect to be used by God to change lives where you work and live. The Christian life is exciting! It's natural to be nervous a little bit. The tragedy is that we can live in our neighborhood for so long and not have an impact on our neighbors. That's not acceptable. We are salt, and we are the light of the world.

God has ideas, and He has abilities. You are gifted by His Spirit. You know the Word. You have Jesus. You have a home. You have a couple of things to spare. Someone might say, "I really have on my heart the ladies in the neighborhood. I want to reach out to moms where I live." Or someone else thinks, "I really want to focus on the kids because the kids bring all of the families out." There are a whole lot of ways to reach your neighbors. The goal is not just to see lives transformed but the Lord to be glorified in our hearts and our lives. The Father promised: if we lift up the name of Jesus, He will draw men to Him. The Spirit does all the work. If we lift Jesus up, He will draw people to Himself. We are co-laborers in His Kingdom. What an honor we have. Do you want to see your community turned upside down for God's Kingdom? There's not much time left. Let us be busy with the work while there's still time to work (John 9:4).

Follow Up
Making Disciples

Sometimes I get the question, "What do you do if you lead someone to the Lord who does not live near you?" Say you're on a trip, and God puts you in the path of someone searching, like with Philip and the eunuch in the Book of Acts. You can't lead them to the Lord and forget them. You can't just abandon them. There are some practical things we can do.

I've had this experience several times. In one instance, after leading a man to Christ, I felt I was responsible for him until he could mature enough to stand on his own. He was naturally looking for help with his new life. He needed direction. He needed a church. I was the one who was discipling him as much as I could until I could lead him into a local church where the pastor could take over the task of discipleship. I gave him some follow-up material, tried to stay present in his life, and not just move on after sharing the Gospel. We need to take a similar approach to those we lead to faith.

This chapter is about follow-up and completing the task of making disciples. Too often, churches focus on either evangelism or discipleship. A balance of both in the church is the fruit of a healthy church.

People experience different crises in their lives. When they encounter such traumas, they're very open to the Gospel. After trying everything else but God and realizing it all has the same dismal end, they're ready to hear His word and respond. The woman with the issue of blood for eighteen years in the Bible is a good example. She was desperate for a touch from the Lord. There are so many people under extreme stress who are looking for help. People are in trouble all around you. When you engage them in a conversation, what are the three things people easily talk about? Family, background, and occupation. Commit yourself to the Lord, and He will direct you, prepare you, and use you to lead others to Himself. The Spirit knows who is ready, and He will show you.

This chapter focuses on follow-up and making disciples. One flows from and into the other. This young man I led to Lord, who lived out of town is an example. I obeyed the Lord. Now, I have a brand-new baby in Jesus on my hands. We need to understand what follow-up is and why it is so crucial. We will discuss "Reaching the Goal" and "Body Ministry." Follow-up and making disciples are two vital streams that join to make a mighty river that flows from evangelism. We will seek to answer the questions: "What is follow-up?" "Why is it crucial?" and "What makes it so significant?" Follow-up and discipleship are not talked about enough in the church. Is it our goal to make converts, or are we commanded to make disciples? It's very obvious what the scriptures teach, but many times we think our only objective is to make a convert. If you are successful in converting a person, then you have someone who is born again. You've only just started. Winning them is only fifty percent of the Great Commission presented in Matthew:

> *Jesus came and told His disciples,*
> *"I have been given all authority in heaven and on earth.*
> *Therefore, go and make disciples of all nations, baptizing them in the name of the Father and the Son and the Holy Spirit. Teach these new disciples to obey all the commands I have given you. And be sure of this: I am with you always, even to the end of the age."*
> Matthew 28:19-20 (NLT)

Verse 18 is the foundation for the commission: "All authority has been given to me in heaven and earth." Jesus is declaring His universal sovereignty—"I have all authority in heaven and earth!" Think about the magnitude of what He's claiming. We're so used to reading the Scriptures over and over that we could really miss the reality of what He's declaring in this verse. Jesus is claiming complete power over everything in the universe! He is affirming Himself as God, the Creator of heaven and earth, as it is repeated in Hebrews and Colossians 1. Jesus is proclaiming, "Because I have all authority in heaven and earth, I'm sending you." On the basis of His ultimate authority over everything and everyone in the universe, He is sending His followers over every century with a specific divine purpose.

Mark's account of this commission says that He went with them, working with them (Mark 16). How does Jesus work with us? Where does Christ live when we're born of the Holy Ghost? Christ is in us (Colossians 1:26). It's no longer we that live but Christ that lives in us (Galatians 2:20). Jesus is commissioning His disciples, deputizing them with His power, declaring, "You have all authority because I'm with you. I'm promising you—giving you divine assurance—I will never leave you or forsake you. I'm asking you to go out and be My representatives with the full assurance of My authority in heaven and earth. Therefore, you go and do as I did because I live in you." He says, "Let's go do the will of the Father! You go, and I'm going to confirm your message with My power. I will work with you!"

Disciples vs. Converts

Isn't that reassuring? The words of Jesus are very encouraging, but the command gets exciting only when we obey it. What is our goal? Is the goal to make converts, or is the goal to make a disciple? Some evangelists are criticized for making only converts. This was a major issue in the early days of Billy Graham's ministry. Follow-up is often neglected by some because it is too hard. Discipleship seems not to be a major focus of many congregations. But what's the church all about? Galatians tells us that when we are born again, we become members of the Household of Faith. It's like giving birth to a baby but never feeding or caring for it. It's up to you and me to care for the newly born again. When you lead another person to Christ, congratulations are in order! Congratulations, you just had a baby. Congrats! Your labor pains of intercession for the past few months have paid off. Your efforts to share your faith have succeeded! Imagine if we were giving birth to just one new believer every year. What if each of us were leading just one other person to Christ each year? Wouldn't that be fantastic! We can do more than that, but how much would the Church grow if we each won one soul each year? This is a worthy goal because each new convert needs to be discipled. If indeed the goal is not just making a convert but is actually making a disciple. This is what Matthew 28 commands.

Four steps are required for us to become mature followers of Jesus Christ. Number One is salvation. We must be born again. Number Two is plugging into the Body. There is no growth without connection with other believers. Number Three is serving. The Christian life is a life modeled after Jesus, Who was the servant of all. Number Four is becoming disciplers. The process of maturity is complete when we have been discipled and, in turn, disciple some else. These four objectives indicate a process. Making a disciple is a process. We know making a convert, someone becoming born again, is the process of the Holy Spirit. We might be just one of the people who shared the Gospel with them, one of the steps along the path of that person's soul to actually being born again. One sows; another waters. We may be a sower, a waterer, or the one to receive the increase. We could be the one who reaps the harvest of a soul for Christ.

What to do After Someone Gets Saved

After someone puts his faith and trust in Christ as his personal Lord and Savior, it's critical to review with them what happened by reinforcing their salvation with scriptures. It becomes extremely critical because suddenly, they have a real enemy who's after their soul. After a while, they might start second-guessing themselves. The emotion they had when they received the Lord may have waned. The enemy may try to put doubt in their mind. Coming to Jesus for the first time can be an emotional experience.

When someone gets saved, what do we want to go over immediately with them? We wish to stress who Jesus is, why Jesus, and what He has done for us. You've already explained all of this in sharing the Gospel. Often in sharing the Gospel, less is more. You don't have to give every single scripture in the Bible that deals with eternal life when you present the Gospel. The Gospel, in a nutshell is Christ died for us, and He rose again. 1 Corinthians 15 is a great summary of the Gospel. The Book of Romans is full of verses you can share. I focus on the words "believe" and "whosoever." When you really focus on "believe" and explain what it means to depend, that is, put our faith and trust in Christ, people will respond. I explained by faith using natural analogies like sitting in a chair. I said, "You sat in that chair. Did you evaluate whether the chair could hold your weight before you sat in it?" Go slow and be patient. One thing leads to another, and the next thing you know, the lights come on in a person's heart. Suddenly, the revelation of the Holy Spirit breaks through, and they understand the Gospel. There is nothing we can do but be used. We don't even have to be ready to share. I have told the Lord more than once, "Wow! You were ready to save that person tonight even though I wasn't!" I was sharing with a young man one time, and he took me to his grandfather's room. He said it was a special place to him. I said, "Pick your spot. This is your night. It's a real special day and time for you." He said, "This is a special room. I always feel something when I come in here." I said, "You're about to feel the real thing tonight." Then he went on to say, "I need to tell you something. I have three tumors in my head. I'm being treated for cancer. You can't tell my grandmother (who was my aunt); she doesn't know. "I started talking about "soteria," wholeness in Spirit, soul, and body. I believe the Lord touched that young man that night. He got the whole package that night. He recognized that he had a bigger problem than the tumors; it is called "sin." He experienced a touch from Jesus.

Why is effective follow-up so necessary? What are some reasons you can think of? Robert Coleman has written a classic book called, The Master Plan of Evangelism. In it, he focuses on how Jesus took twelve people and committed His time and energy to them. They were the first disciples. The first thing you see in the example of Christ and how He discipled the original twelve apostles is He committed himself to them. He selected them and chose these twelve men to spend the most time with. He did not commit Himself to everybody. Mark relates that Jesus called the twelve to Himself and appointed them that they should be with Him. I love that statement. They were saved to Christ. We lose sight of why they were saved. They were saved by Him and for Him. He chose them for His purpose. He appointed them to know the Lord—for His glory. He called them "to Himself." Jesus went through great pain on the cross and shed His blood so that they could be reconciled to Him. He made them one with God and restored them to relationship with the Creator of all heaven and earth.

New believers are vulnerable because they often don't know much about what happened to them. I remember a young lady we led to the Lord at Cracker Barrel. She was ripe for the Gospel. She was a young lady in her early twenties. I was not going to personally disciple her because she was a woman. I thought it would be best if my wife did. She had a real need for friendship, especially friends who believed in Jesus, because she did not have any. She had an equal need for affirmation. She needed to have people surround her with love and care to help her grow in her relationship with Christ. Unfortunately, she had a close friend who professed to be a Christian but lived a hypocritical life. That friend was not a good example for her. This young lady had received the Lord. She was under conviction for her lifestyle. She was pursuing holiness. She began going to church and reading her Bible. God was doing a work in her, and her friend would tell her, "You don't really have to do what Jesus says. God understands that we are all human." She was being used by the devil to work against her faith. We have to trust the power of God to finish what He began in that person's life. The Holy Spirit is active and present, but people need support from other people who will lead them in a way that is productive and safe. New believers are vulnerable to the lies of the enemy. She was vulnerable, and unless she was shown the way, she would have probably chosen her old fleshly ways. There is a difference between salvation and renewing of the mind. The Gospel can't be changed because people get offended. We have to hold fast to the profession of our faith (Hebrews 10:23).

Jesus told those who wanted to follow Him, "Unless you eat My flesh and drink My blood, you can't be My disciple" (John 6). Today, we have softened the demands. Jesus did not. He laid it on pretty thick. He was upfront about the cost of discipleship. Luke 9 says, "If anyone wants to be My disciple, let him deny himself, pick up his cross, and follow Me daily." He did not make it easy. It's a process. Discipleship is a progression. Those who disciple need patience much more than they think. Discipling people takes time. We need God's grace to mentor people.

The Bible says Satan goes about like a roaring lion. The enemy comes in like a flood. New Christians don't know how to raise up the standard and use the Scripture as an offensive weapon. They can be vulnerable to false doctrine. They can have someone who comes to them and invites them to a group that is not Scripturally based. New Christians, because they have such a potential to change, can also be too open to new things. They don't have the ability to discern spiritually yet. They've received the Lord, and they want to change to be conformed to Him. When they encounter this new life, they can go either way. Usually, they step in the right direction. When they are discipled properly, they follow Jesus. However, even though they are new babes in Christ, the Holy Spirit reveals in them right and wrong. Even though they may not be able to point to it in their Bibles, the Holy Spirit leads Christians, young and old, into all truth.

Personal follow-up increases the effectiveness of their spiritual development. You will run into people who haven't been properly discipled. They are nowhere near where they could be. Some of you have met Christians who have been walking with the Lord for many, many years. The difference between the mature and those still acting like babies is the mature have been discipled, often by good pastors and by being a part of a Bible-believing and Bible-living church. What may seem a normal Biblical response to a seasoned believer is not to everyone. Many who have professed Christ are not renewing their minds. They lack a consistent reading and studying of the Scriptures. They lack awareness of good Bible doctrine and sound theology. They don't have good spiritual standing. They are more apt to be "tossed to and fro," as James says. Believers have a heart for the Lord and love God, but too many are getting slapped around way more than they should by circumstances and demons.

This is what that baptism of power is for. The Great Commission is based on the authority of our Lord Jesus Christ. We are sent in His power.

The 120 were commanded by Jesus to wait. They were to wait for the promise of the power of the Holy Spirit. They were baptized in His power and granted His authority. They did not serve in their own power. Dependence on the Holy Spirit makes our evangelism more effective, increasing the multiplication factor and making us more effective with our witness. When we share the Gospel under the power of the Holy Spirit, people know we genuinely care for them because they sense the love of God coming through us.

Discipleship Requires Relationship

Genuine, authentic relationships can't be felt online. No one online can lay hands on you, hug you, or be there to cry with you when you cry or rejoice with you when you rejoice. That is not how God intended the church to function, according to the Scriptures. Yes, the Internet gives greater access to get the Gospel out and reach lives with the Word of God, but it's not a substitute for being plugged into a church family. When we disciple people, we see that they have a good church family, surrounded by strong, mature believers—a family made up of moms and dads and brothers and sisters in Christ. Their growth is expedited in the atmosphere of the loving family of God under Biblical guidance through God-given ministers, according to Ephesians. They don't have to go around the same mountain as the Israelites did in the Old Testament. They are learning from the successes and failures of others. A work of sanctification takes place, a practical work of sanctification, not just a positional one. They're already sanctified in Jesus and redeemed by the blood of the Lamb, but they're practically learning the lifestyle of Jesus, and His character becomes available to them. They are growing into the image and lifestyle of Christ. His life is being formed in them in a healthy manner (Galatians 5:22-24). Discipled people aren't constantly experiencing the same roadblocks over and over. As Scripture says, they are laying aside the weights and sins that so easily ensnare them. Discipled people grow in Christ.

We define the follow-up process as:

> *The process of giving continued attention to new Christians until they are at home in a local church, until they find out how they can serve, until they can develop the character of Christ (until they learn how to pursue Christlikeness on their own until they know how to get into the Word and pursue the voice of God in their lives), and until they can help to build Christ's Church by discipling others.*

The keywords in this definition are "the process of giving continued attention." That's what it takes. Disciples want to be discipled. If they cease desiring discipleship, we need to go back to the salvation message. People who have been born again want to grow into the image of Jesus. It can be messy depending on the life that a person was saved out of. Sanctification works through people differently. We need to give continued attention to the newly born again so they can have the assistance they need to grow.

It's imperative that we are sharing the Gospel with ourselves. I may say I believe in salvation by grace alone. I may even preach it, but if I relate to God based on works and not through faith from my heart, I'm going to communicate that when I mentor somebody. I am going to expect them to perform at a certain level that God does not require. If I'm not patient, I will get frustrated with their development. It becomes a real hindrance and produces Pharisees.

I led a young man to the Lord one time, and the change was evident. He asked me a fantastic question. He said he used to be into science, and he thought that science would always conflict with religion. I said, "Not at all. True science will reinforce what the Bible declares." He said, "Man, I thought that!" as he was investigating. I said, "Absolutely!" And asked, "Are you into that? I have some material I'll send you that will be a real blessing to you; it will knock your socks off. While doing that, why don't you check out the resurrection scientifically, look for the scientific facts into it." True science will always point to God, whether it's the law of thermodynamics or patterns in the ocean. If you are honest, any scientific study will ultimately lead you to God. What science is just now discovering, the Bible declared a long time ago. It is important how we mentor because how we think will be reflected in how we disciple. To maintain focus, we won't give examples of that here.

Many churches need help in the area of follow-up. It's what evangelists often prepare churches to do to get ready for crusades. It also leaves the most lasting impact on a community. It trains the churches to reach out in ways they may not have before. It's a challenge for pastors and local churches to assimilate new believers into their activities. Too many pastors are quoted as saying, "The back door of the church is much larger than the front door." They say this because their efforts to disciple are weak. Different churches have different emphases. Some churches are very effective in the introduction. They concentrate on winning souls and introducing people to Jesus. They're good at evangelism. They're good at leading souls to Christ but very imbalanced in their discipleship. Other churches are very strong on discipleship but very weak on introduction and evangelizing new souls. How do you see yourself as an individual in the church? How do you view your church in light of the four objectives? Thank God, there are churches and ministries that are balanced, but they are rare.

My home church, where I'm an elder, is strong on discipleship, yet we are a sending church. Discipleship training is a major part of what we do. It is a big part of our business. 2 Timothy 2:2 calls us to commit to faithful men who are able to teach others. This is the hallmark passage. You're going to have a lot fewer souls to disciple if you don't keep having babies. What are we going to do, stop evangelizing so we can disciple? Many churches are losing members. Membership and church attendance are down in the US. Some churches have gotten rid of membership altogether. They think church is just a place where we go to fellowship. They want the doors open to everybody. Some have members but don't know if those members are saved or not.

The early church took literally what Christ said. What happened to the Ethiopian eunuch is an example. Phillip asks, "Can anyone forbid that he should be baptized?" A pattern has developed from this account. When someone believes, they are then baptized in water. Baptism is something we need to teach and practice because it's scriptural. Baptism is important for new followers of Christ. You want to discuss that with those whom you are discipling.

What are some of the main aspects of follow-up? What steps are important so a young babe can experience spiritual growth? One of the first things is to teach the assurance of salvation. We need to reinforce the reality that faith is assured in Jesus Christ. I encourage new converts to memorize John 5:24: "Verily, verily, I say unto you, He that heareth my word, and believeth on him that sent me, hath everlasting life, and shall not come into condemnation; but is passed from death unto life."

How did he avoid judgment, and how is he assured of eternal life? It was through believing. That Greek word for believe is used ninety times in John's Gospel alone. Believing in Christ gave him the assurance of his salvation. The enemy is going to come in and plant seeds of doubt. New believers are going to be confronted with temptations. They still have a long journey of renewing their minds. They need to have some behavior modification. They need to flee youthful lusts. They need to shun the appearance of evil. They don't need to be conformed to this world but transformed by the renewing of their minds. They need to heed the call of Jesus, "He who sins, sin no more.

Go and sin no more lest a worse thing happen to you." It is a matter of faith, not works. The motive is not to earn God's approval. That's the wrong motive because we already have His acceptance in Christ. We're already loved. We don't have to earn it. We have it. It is natural for you to want to love Him back and honor Him with your life. He enables us to "be all we can be" in Jesus. At first, memorization is a key aspect to renewing your mind because you are learning about your assurance. Bible memorization aids in the renewing of the mind.

Important Aspects for New Believers

Another important aspect is the church and relationships. The church is where we concentrate our fellowship. The local body is where we connect and relate to other believers, where believers are edified by each other's service and gifts. The Scriptures are also vital for our discipleship. Daily reading the Word is how we renew our minds. In addition, accountability to another person is how we grow best. When someone plugs into the body, there are natural points where some are made accountable. Some churches have small groups or "connect groups" because they help facilitate interaction and personal care. They may be faithful to come to church and hear the sermon, but getting people connected with one another is a challenge, especially in our American culture.

Many churches want to disciple people. The importance of Scriptures is a major part of discipling. Daily reading and study of the Word are crucial for spiritual growth. The Bible says to study to show yourself approved unto God. Memorizing the Word is a huge aid to absorbing the Word into your heart and mind. These are key disciplines of the Christian faith, all having to do with the Word: reading the Word, studying the Word, memorizing the Scriptures, praying, meditation, and fasting. Memorization, especially for young believers, is important for renewing the mind (Romans 12:1-2). It makes whatever area of temptation they are walking through easier to overcome. Absorbing the Word in your life enables deliverance from things in the past and gives hope for the future as faith begins to grow.

The promise of the Holy Spirit carried the power to be witnesses. "You shall be My witnesses." These are ways of growing. Memorize Scripture to renew the mind. Young converts need to be aware that just because they got saved doesn't mean they're not going to have temptations. In fact, it can just be the beginning of more temptation. Is temptation sin? That's a good question many get tangled up with. Learn to distinguish between sin and temptation. Has anyone ever asked you, "Can I pray too much? Do I get a time slot with God, and that's my only time?" or "Is it bad to pray in the shower?" They ask because they are naked. They think it may be a bad thing, an impure prayer. The Bible says to pray without ceasing. Tell them to turn to 1 Thessalonians 5:17. It takes three minutes of your time. Often the new convert is like a baby. Answer their questions, and they're on their happy, merry way. Three days later, they might call you with another question, or you might just check on them. You get hilarious questions. The young man I told you about once asked, "How were they saved in the Old Testament?" How were people saved in the Old Testament that didn't have Christ? That's a good question. I showed him what the Bible said about it: very simply, the same way, by faith (Romans 1:17 and 4:3).

We need to help new believers learn to discern God's will. The prophet Elijah waited to hear God's voice in the Book of Kings, Chapter 19. How do I know God's will? How do I know if I'm going in the right direction? You don't have to give them every single scripture in the Bible. They're babes; they're going to build on their faith. They're going to get more renewed in different areas. The Bible is the revealed will of God for young converts to learn about. Scriptures give inner peace. The Word provides counsel for every part of your life.

Abiding in the Lord is another important area to teach new converts. What does abiding in Christ mean? What does that look like? Abiding in Christ involves the pursuit of the Kingdom, applying the Word of God, and growing in the character of Christ. Go over with each new believer these things repetitively, patiently, slowly, methodically, meeting with them weekly. Being a good listener is a very important part of discipleship. When a person gets saved, you should try to meet them within a couple of days. If you cannot meet face to face, follow up with a phone call and meet up again as soon as possible. You should be having a sit-down with their family, meeting with them at their house. Yes, go out of your way. "I'll see you at church in two weeks"—I've done that and seen it fail. That's not what they need. It's not the wisest approach. It is not sin, but it is not wise to leave a baby Christian unattended after he gets saved.

Needs of New Believers

New Christians have some basic needs, and here are some. They need spiritual food (1 Peter). They need love, encouragement, prayer, and acceptance despite their sins, failures, and weaknesses. They are going to make mistakes. Some people work harder at trying not to make a mistake than they do at "going for it" because they're scared to make a mistake. When I hire people, I tell them if you're working hard, you're going to make mistakes. If you're trying to learn this job, you're going to make mistakes. I'd rather have them make mistakes from trying too hard than have them not try at all. It means you're trying. Some people approach evangelism like that. They say, "I'm scared of being a bad Christian, so I'm not going to be one at all." Fear of failure paralyzes them.

New Christians need protection. They need nurturing and care. They need fellowship (1 Peter 5:8). Studies have shown that friendship and acceptance are two of the main reasons that people maintain fellowship in a church. You might say, "Well, if they're saved, that shouldn't matter." Well, are you one of those giving them acceptance and nurture? If they're really born again, friendship and fellowship shouldn't matter. If they don't make new friends, they're likely not to stay in church. Friendships help us maintain relationship with God.

Everyone needs a sense of community. Sometimes common interests and common backgrounds can be helpful. Most of the people may not be of your generation or your socio-economic class. It doesn't mean you can't reach out, but you do. You reach out and do what you can initially. Someone else might benefit from knowing you and becoming your friend. Friendship is practical and real. Colossians 2:6-7 talks about being rooted, grounded, and strengthened in the faith. Such depth takes time, and the entire church plays a vital role in a person becoming rooted, grounded, and strengthened. It's a process. It takes all-hands-on-deck for real community to happen.

Another thing a new believer needs is purpose and ministry. Everyone needs to feel they are needed; that's where serving comes in. When a new believer gets plugged into serving, he is motivated to grow. Challenge young converts to serve others, give them an opportunity to serve, and want to be a part of the body. Growing believers need people to pray for them. They need to hear and to know, "I'm praying for you." People sincerely concerned about them can ask, "How are you doing? How's that new job?" All we have to do is pray and check on them. Don't wait for someone else to do it. What if you're twice their age—you're a mom; you're a dad? Reach out like they're your own kid. Talk to them with that same love of Jesus. If they're older than you and they look like your parents, then reach out to them. They're a grandparent, "Hey, I'm here to help you with anything." Encourage them lovingly.

Building relationships through the process of follow-up naturally facilitates discipleship. It's the early groundwork of discipling. Then comes body ministry, the need to build relationships and friendships to integrate them into the community. It becomes a way of life. There is an integration into the community. That's where that "believe, belong behavior pattern" comes in. It is not focusing on "belonging, behavior, and then belief." We don't say, "If you behave in a certain way and you plug into the church this way, then I know you have belief." True belief comes first. The right message, the right salvation, and the right Gospel lead to mature believers.

Discipleship is the whole process of new believers learning and growing in their salvation. Discipleship is getting new believers plugged into the household of faith, becoming servants of others, and being disciplers. Matthew 28:20 (paraphrased) says: "Teach these new disciples to obey all the commands I have given you. And be sure of this: I am with you always, even to the end."

This is discipleship: teaching them. Teach these new disciples to obey all the commands. That is discipleship. Follow-up is critical for many of the reasons we discussed. Following up naturally leads to discipleship.

The Father loves us. He called us out of darkness and into His marvelous light. The Father imparted (shared with us and put inside us) His divine nature. We're sons and daughters and one with the Godhead—co-equals, heirs, and joint heirs with Christ. Let's give Him all the glory as we follow up and disciple those God uses us to help be reconciled to Him.

Time to Step Up The Spirit @ Work

God created us in Christ Jesus for good works, and those good works produce eternal fruit. The fruit of our lives is other souls that we share the Gospel with. Sharing our faith is a big part of the eternal fruit that each one of us is to produce. If we are separating our jobs from our relationship with God, we are missing a big part of what God intended for us. One-third of our lives is spent in the workplace, and I believe this is where God wants us to make an eternal impact. Evangelism is not a program; it is a lifestyle. It is loving others with the same love we receive from God through Christ. It's relying on the Holy Spirit of Christ to lead us and work through us. Ministry is not the vocation of just paid clergy. Every believer in Jesus Christ is called to fulfill the Great Commission. What better place to do it than where God has planted you?

The workplace, whether it be an office or construction site, is an environment where we can let our light shine. We can impact our coworkers like no full-time preacher can. When we come home from work, are we impacting our neighbors? Are we impacting other parts of the community? Our communities are full of lives that we can connect with through a service we provide in our own business. One of mine was my barbershop salon environment. Your corporate setting could be in a cubicle, at a desk, or on a job site. What better way to serve God and reach people than to use the place you spend eight hours a day?

It requires Kingdom motives to reach the lives around us. This is what makes followers of Christ different from other people. We do the same jobs everyone else does, but we are working for the glory of God and the advancement of His Kingdom. God wants to do those things through us right where you are. Why we do what we do should be the key difference (Deuteronomy 8:18). All ability to obtain wealth comes from God and should be viewed as establishing His covenant and building His Kingdom. This will help build strong churches. God wants to do powerful things through us because Christ lives in us. He is the evangelist. He is the soul-winner, and He is the compassionate one. If we block Him out of our lives because we are blinded from seeing our jobs as our mission, we miss why He put us where we are. Our attitude towards our work sets the tone for how we succeed according to the Kingdom of Heaven. We must see our job as the first and foremost mission field in our lives. If God's mission is not our mission, and we do His mission only on Sundays but not at work, not in our neighborhood, something is fundamentally off.

Jesus Christ is to be the Lord of all, every day, all the time. His Spirit has placed us where we are for His purposes. Our work provides for our families and us, but our job is also the place God has called many of us and where the Spirit has equipped us to serve others best and bring glory to God. We must see the workplace differently to change the world.

I have been an entrepreneur for decades now. By God's grace, I have established salons, barbershops, and restaurants, all conceived to impact people's lives and the community. My approach is to directly and indirectly reach people with the Gospel of the Kingdom. We have "Don's Wood-Fired Pizza" as an outpost since 2005. Before that, we spent ten years in Tysons Corner, Virginia, reaching lives through International Barbers. We sold that business after I injured my back and went through a physical trial. We ultimately expanded into another location, and God blessed us with a field white for harvest. The blessings came because of a good work ethic and putting God first. We offered professional services and products at a fair price.

Most importantly, we chose a strategic location for sharing the Gospel of the Kingdom that included salvation, but we also saw the Lord work miracles that drew people to Christ. Many lives have been impacted. We shared the Gospel for ten years in Tysons Corner with hundreds of people.

Through our businesses, we build relationships and look for opportunities to reach the community. At the Tyson's Corner hair salon, we hired people who wanted to learn to use their chair and their services as their pulpit. Our objective was to honor the Lord. We also had direct outreaches and Bible studies from the business. Our Bible studies are still going on now, and workers and customers are being impacted daily. We visit a juvenile detention center every quarter, where we hold pizza celebrations, give away Bibles, have discussions, share testimonies, and minister in worship music. Though they may not be ready to attend church, some of those residents remember the relationship and the impact we had on them when they were released. They came to visit us at the restaurant. I hired one of them the other day. He is a young man who is working with us now. He came to me after his release and said, "Do you remember me?" I said, "Yes, how are you doing?" He lives near the business. He is just one whom we have reached by seeing our job as our ministry.

Once a business is set up to enable people to advance the Kingdom through their everyday activity, it becomes an amazing tool to impact hundreds and thousands of lives. There are innumerable ways to touch lives through our jobs and businesses. We sponsor a school to build relationships. We equip and challenge our staff who are believers to use their jobs as their mission field. We deal with suppliers almost every day, every one of whom gets a slice of pizza and a drink on the house. They tell us, "This is our favorite stop. We look forward to coming here." We give them devotionals as gifts and Gospel tracts. I pray with several of them. Every quarter, a company comes to clean the restaurant's grease traps—that's a dirty job! Once, they sent a new worker who arrived before the restaurant had opened. We had a great conversation, and within a few minutes, he was on his knees in front of the espresso machine receiving Christ as his Lord and Savior. He was so receptive, as the Holy Spirit was clearly dealing with him. If we put ourselves in position for God to use us, He will. We must see our jobs and worksites as our mission field.

Work provides a constant source of people who need to hear the message of God's love for them. Work allows us to meet people in the community, whether it is a customer, a business-to-business meeting, or people you are doing business with (purveyors, suppliers, marketers, and more). All the aspects of a business can be opportunities for advancing the Kingdom. We even build relationships with the bank and its staff. Bringing in a free pizza opens the door for us to tell them, "Thank you for your service." Expressing gratitude for people and what they do and looking for opportunities to be kind build trust so we can pray for their needs.

We are agents of God's love; we are agents of the Holy Spirit. God resides in us; He wants to live through us everywhere we go, especially the workplace. We spend so much time with coworkers. We are there to give 100 percent of our effort, and our testimony should reflect Christ's love for them through us. Whatever we do, we do as unto the Lord. Scripture instructs us to do everything with all our hearts as unto the Lord. The testimony of our work ethic is a start, but it is not complete. We still need to show we care and share the message of God's love.

There are some very disciplined professional people in the workplace who can outperform what we do on the job. If hard work is the only measure of godliness, we are in trouble! The world can do that. The difference is God's love through us for them. The difference has to be the motive behind what I do. Do I see my job as my pulpit? Do I view it as an opportunity to serve my fellow man?

The greatest commandment is to love God with all your heart, mind, soul, and strength. The second is love your neighbor as yourself. If we are not loving God properly, we are not going to love our neighbor. We cannot love God properly without loving our neighbor. 1 John 4 says, "Do not say you love me, whom you cannot see, and not love your brother, who you can see." There are plenty of opportunities to reciprocate God's love to others. What often holds us back is our over-analysis of ourselves beyond what the Scripture declares. Self-analysis creates paralysis. It stops us from moving forward and growing with God. It freezes our progress in the love of God, so we don't share His love and hope that we have experienced in our lives. Turn to God and say, "God, I cannot do this, but You can. God, I cannot love my fellow man properly, but You can. God, I cannot be a missionary here on the job, but You can. Teach me, Lord."

We need godly wisdom. Proverbs says, "He who wins souls is wise." The Lord knows how to reach the people He places around us to serve. Paul said, "I serve them that I might win them" (1 Corinthians 9). Service is a great opportunity to open the door of people's hearts to the Gospel. Each environment God put us in has unique elements that we can use to the glory of God. When we look to the Lord for wisdom and how to reach people, we learn it often starts best with a simple act of kindness. Genuinely caring for our fellow man and our coworkers is a good place to start. It's easy! Just ask, "How are you? How is it going? How are your wife and kids doing? Are you okay? Have you been staying healthy?" etc.

Why are we asking? No one else may care, but we do. We all go to work, go through the grind, pretending we are happy, and then leave to go home. We come back the next day and do it all over again. Don't be a pretender. Our love is to be genuine, not fake. People pick up on whether we are real or not. They don't have to be told what real love looks like. If we do not respond to someone right away, especially in their times of trouble, we may miss an opportunity to reflect the love of God to him.

I have heard testimony after testimony of this at work. I have seen in my own life when a hurting, lost person seeks out a coworker who is a believer.

WHY NOT YOU?

A neighbor in my neighborhood lost her mother. The family came out of nowhere and asked me to perform the funeral service. I have been praying for that neighborhood. The family told me that they wanted the service to be performed by someone who knew their mom. I really didn't know her or the family that well. I just loved them by being cordial to the family whenever I saw them. They were very nice people. Since then, the oldest son has given his life to Christ and attends our church.

We may never realize the impact we are having on someone. Most of the other neighbors are too busy to care for each other or have never taken the time to take an interest. Loving our neighbor can be as simple as taking time to notice them. It is the little things. People notice. Kindness opens doors for greater expressions of His love. We can invite our neighbors over to our house. We can see if they need anything. The Bible says, "Your neighbor lives next to you for safety." You may be the only believer they know and trust.

This book is not a "how-to." It is not a theological treatise on evangelism or missions. It is simply the heart's cry of a simple follower of Christ who desires to share what God has done with him. Although I am educated, most of what I have learned about sharing the Gospel has been from experience and being discipled by others. I have learned by doing. This is one of the central problems I wish to address in this book. I passionately desire to encourage people to do evangelism! I know some might think my way is not the best or correct method, but I like to think that what I am doing is still better than what most people are NOT doing. Most believers do not share their faith every day. Most have never shared in their entire Christian life!

This book speaks to every believer, encouraging him to step out in faith and share the love of Jesus with everyone, everywhere, every day. By virtue of the presence of the Holy Spirit in the life of a follower of Christ, we are empowered with everything we need to be a witness. We are empowered with all the power we need to be agents of transformation in this hurting world. Through the Holy Spirit, every Christian is enabled with special grace to serve God and his fellow man with unique gifts that present the invisible God to man in real and tangible ways. You can do this because this is what you were created for.

God has sent me on a journey from death to life, and I like life so much better than death. I have experienced the love of God at a depth so profound that I will never be able to express it or pay Him back. I wrote this book to encourage you to let God use you to change your world right where He has planted you. I have written it so anyone can understand it. You do not have to be a Bible scholar to do the will of God. In fact, most will never minister in a formal position. But everyone can serve where God has put him. Join me on this adventure of love to see how the Spirit is at work and how He can work through you. Bless you as you seek to fulfill your calling to reach everyone, everywhere, every day with the Gospel.

About the Author

Waleed Zarou is an ordained evangelist through Calvary Temple Ministries. Waleed has over 30 years of leadership and ministry. Waleed has developed and been instrumental in creating effective gospel outreach strategies in the US and abroad. While part of the national Mike Hines crusades in Central America, he may be best known for founding International Barbers and The Dons Wood-Fired Pizza businesses for missions. Waleed either holds a degree or certificate or attended one of the following institutions, including Montgomery College, University of Maryland, University of Central Florida, Temple University, Graham Webb Academy, Berean School of the Bible, Global University, Vanguard University, Dallas Theological Seminary, Biola University, and Moody Bible Institute. Waleed continues to be interviewed for radio and TV and is a guest at conferences. He is also an ordained Chaplain and has served in various prisons and public service sectors.

EvgWaleedZarou@gmail.com

 WaleedZarou

 WaleedZarou-Evangelist

All proceeds from the sale of this book go to support Open Hearts ministry.

www.WaleedZarou.com

www.ingramcontent.com/pod-product-compliance
Lightning Source LLC
LaVergne TN
LVHW061618070526
838199LV00078B/7327